Wisdom Seeking:

Thirty Days with the
Book of Proverbs

Wisdom Seeking:

Thirty Days with the Book of Proverbs

William R. Long
MDiv, PhD, JD

For Katherine,
whose life provided
much of this book,
esp. ch. 20.
Thank you for all your
support —
Bill Long

Inquiries should be addressed to:
William R. Long

www.drbilllong.com
drbilllong@gmail.com

ISBN 1449534716
EAN 9781449534714

cover and book design by Jerri Strozier

"Whoever finds me, finds life,"
Proverbs 8:35

CONTENTS

Proverbs That Are Too Good To Miss

Preface

WE LIVE OUR LIVES between Job and Proverbs. The Book of Job explores a life that has fallen apart, while Proverbs exposits the life that is complete or whole. Job is about the "fractured" life; Proverbs explores the life of "integrity." Job explores the life of chaos; Proverbs is interested in an ordered life. Job is a cry of pain; Proverbs is a call to predictability. Job's complaint is that faithful living cannot protect you from chaos; Proverbs is convinced that faithful living leads to avoidance of chaos.

Yet, despite the seeming contrariety of the values of these two stunning books, both seem to reflect something of the other in their work. Even though he is plunged into confusion and deep distress, Job longs for the kind of ordered life that Proverbs promises. And, in an arresting change of fortune, at the end of the book he is given a double share of everything he had when he was most prosperous (Job 42:10). Even though Proverbs presents, in memorable aphorisms, the value and joy of the ordered life, occasionally it lets slip a verse that shows that life is sometimes just a losing proposition. "Even in laughter the heart is sad, and the end of joy is grief," Prov. 14:13.

Yet there the two books remain, like two arresting monoliths, as they emphasize two different sides of the "coin" of life. Or, to change the metaphor, they represent two curbstones that confine the road of life down which we travel. Sometimes, when life overwhelms or threatens to undo us, we veer more towards the Joban "curb" of life. Other times, when order, predictability and victory is ours, the words of Proverbs tend to capture our experience. We never seem to have experienced fully the desperate straits of Job (though it sometimes feels we have); nor does the seemingly calm confidence in a steady upward climb of Proverbs always characterize us. We live our lives between Job and Proverbs.[1]

The book you have in your hands deals with the "Proverbs side" of the road. It aims at a faithful and full description of the goodness that can result from the ordered life. It argues that at the heart of the Biblical concept of wisdom is the belief that life can be mastered or managed, and that happiness results from applying a series of identifiable principles or rules that lead to life-mastery. By saying that these principles are identifiable does *not* mean that they are easy. In fact, Proverbs is quite committed to what we might call "life as discipline." Discipline will require a great deal of us—in humility, in learning how to shape our words, in learning infinite patience, in learning how to deal with fools and mockers.

In saying that Proverbs teaches that life can be mastered,

---

1   I have written three books on Job (1995, 1997, 2004); this is my first on Proverbs. The two on Job that shed light on Job's psychology are *Trusting God Again: Regaining Hope after Disappointment or Loss* (InterVarsity, 1995); and *A Hard-Fought Hope: Journeying with Job through Mystery* (Upper Room Books, 2004).

I don't mean to say that it teaches that life thereby is dull or uncreative. Quite the contrary. Proverbs itself, as I will show in chapter 1, is aware of the tremendous complexities of life, and it probes these complexities through a number of pithy paradoxical statements that demand the most of our creative interpretive abilities to comprehend. Proverbs teaches clear principles, to be sure, but it does so through guiding us to "think through" some of life's knottiest problems.

USING THIS BOOK

I have written this book for those who would like to become wise or wiser than they now are. I have tried to make each chapter accessible to the general reader as well as challenging to one who has had a lot of experience in studying the Bible. The format is as follows: after three introductory chapters, which describe certain literary and idea features of the Book of Proverbs, I then present 30 brief expositions of selected themes in Proverbs, arranged around five topics. The topics, longing for wisdom, wisdom as a matter of the heart, meet the fool, the way of wisdom, and proverbs that are too good to miss, bring you into the flow of Proverbs as well as into the individual words of many proverbs. These chapters are meant to be a "one a day" diet for 30 days. The one a day format was chosen so that you can engage in the sort of discipline which Proverbs would recognize (a steady course of learning) as well as have time to consider your reaction to each idea I present. Many of the chapters take apart an individual proverb word by word; several of the chapters deal with historical (e.g., the family history of a friend; Day 20) or literary topics (e.g., the fool in Western literature, Day 9). Some chapters make contributions to educational theory (Day 27) or even the study of Abraham

Lincoln's biography (Day 25); one relates a dream I had (Day 4). Each one, however, takes quite seriously the language and flow of the Book of Proverbs.

Throughout the book I use "he" or "she" interchangeably, because the path of wisdom taught by Proverbs isn't just open to one gender. Thus, in one chapter the fool might be a "he," while the next chapter the fool is a "she." God has seemingly so ordered the world that foolishness, as well as wisdom, doesn't seem to be gender-dependent.

I believe there is no task more important to our peace of mind in an increasingly complex and busy world than to attain wisdom. Wisdom anchors our life when the tough and confusing winds blow all around us. Proverbs says, "For the wise the path of life leads upward," 15:24. May that be your experience in reading this book.

I would like to thank the Community Congregational Church of Garden City, KS and especially a conference fund set up by Mrs. Mary Connors, in memory of her husband, for the support to undertake the task of writing this book. I think that partnerships between congregations and scholars/writers in creating materials for study and learning is the key to the development of vital religious life and to understanding better the world around us. To that congregation and the many wonderful people who have cared for me over the past three years in Garden City, I am supremely grateful. Finally, I am deeply grateful for the creative and thoughtful design work and editorial help of Ms. Jerri Strozier (www.lifestoriesinc.com) in putting this manuscript in an attractive and inviting form.

Biblical quotations are from the New Revised Standard Version unless otherwise indicated.

Part One

An Introduction to Proverbs

Chapter One

THE PARADOXES AND PLEASURES
OF THE BOOK OF PROVERBS

A FEW MONTHS AGO I was dining with a friend at a chic new restaurant in Portland, Oregon. I asked him, an accomplished attorney, a diligent student of the Scriptures and a deep thinker about life, what he thought about the Book of Proverbs. To my surprise, he said he didn't study it at all.

"Why?" I inquired.

"Two reasons," he responded. "First, it doesn't major on the significant themes that the rest of the Bible emphasizes, such as the mercy and love of God, forgiveness, or even the covenant between God and the people; and second, because the scope of advice given to the young people in Proverbs is pretty standard or customary."

I pondered his answer for a minute before responding. "If I could make a credible argument that Proverbs is, in fact, about central issues in life, and that, rather than giving pedestrian

1

advice, Proverbs probes nuance and paradox in life, would your attitude about Proverbs change?"

A look of bemused interest creased his face. "Yes, it would," he responded. "I would take it up in an instant."

AN APPROACH TO PROVERBS

My friend's comments had an unexpected effect on me. I had already developed the argument in my mind about the paradoxes or internal tensions in Proverbs, which I will lay out as this chapter progresses, but I hadn't really thought about how best to present that argument in the book. I had "assumed" that the way you do things is to present an introduction to the text, the types of proverbs in the book, the main themes of Proverbs, etc. in the first chapter. After all, *everyone* who writes a book on Proverbs begins with a chapter on textual and thematic issues. Then, I would write on the "paradoxes" of Proverbs.

But my friend's comments cut me short. If his opinion about Proverbs was shared by many people, then most potential readers won't even get to (original) chapter two—the chapter on paradox. They would just put the book down after the "predictable" first chapter. Thus, I had to shift my thinking and present Proverbs as a book of complexity and nuance *before* I even did the standard introductory stuff. As the (non-biblical!) proverb says, "You only get one chance to make a first impression." Thus, I wanted to give a "first impression" of Proverbs that dealt with issues of nuance, paradox and contemporary life rather than the standard issues everyone considers—issues which assume that everyone who reads Proverbs wants to study the book as a committed biblical scholar.

The thesis of this chapter is that Proverbs is a book of wise sayings and sage advice that not only is aware of the paradoxes, tensions or contradictions of life but also presents different aspects of these tensions through its pithy statements. Differently said, Proverbs is like a multi-faceted jewel which, when held up to light at different angles, yields the most stunning prismatic light patterns. In fact, my argument will be that Proverbs takes on some of the central issues of life in seemingly contradictory ways so that it might aid us and encourage us in thinking of how we deal with these imponderables today. By so doing, Proverbs becomes a resource for endless hours of pleasure and instruction, for rumination about our own motives as we teach, learn, and respond to people, and for stimulating thought when we need to be brought out of the humdrum categories of our conventional thinking. Thus, rather than being the agent or expression of pedestrian thinking, Proverbs is, in fact, the instrument through which we break out of limited thought. In the final analysis, Proverbs functions as an engine for theological and practical thought, a stimulus to our own deepening engagement with ideas and with the array of people and situations we encounter in life.

ENTERING THE PARADOXES

A paradox is an apparent contradiction in terms. An example: "The people who arrive earliest are those who drive slowest." C.S. Lewis uttered his famous paradox, with respect to the Narnia series, "Some day you will be old enough to start reading fairly tales again." Again, "Knowledge is a paradox; the more you know, the more you realize you don't know." Paradoxes can be true; indeed, they are arresting precisely because they are unexpectedly true. My contention here is that the Book of Proverbs attempts to deal with several important conundrums or

3

paradoxes in life by articulating different approaches to facets of the paradox. The paradoxes of Proverbs can best be understood by posing questions, which allow two kinds of answers: "Yes and no" or "In two apparently contrary ways." Let me show you what I mean.

ANSWERING THE FOOL

A practical, and very important, question in life is how you deal with people who are slightly or completely foolish. I will introduce the fool in depth in the following chapters, but suffice it to say for now that a fool, generally, is an impulsive person who really has a hard time listening to others. A fool is more interested on hearing his/her own opinion than in considering that of others. Proverbs is convinced that the world is populated by many, many fools. Foolishness can come out in various forms and places. Your boss can be foolish; the speaker at a public gathering can be foolish; someone who is responding to your advice might be foolish. How do you react when you are confronted with the ever-present reality of foolishness in your midst? Proverbs gives the following paradoxical answer:

"Do not answer fools according to their folly,
    or you will be a fool yourself.
Answer fools according to their folly,
    or they will be wise in their own eyes," 26:4-5.

Thus, according to Proverbs, do you answer a person who is spouting foolishness? Yes and No. By presenting the paradox in these contrary formulations, Proverbs encourages thought and conversation. I will explore this topic more fully in Day 11 below, but a few questions these verses provoke are: How have I reacted when confronted with foolishness? Do I keep silent? Confront the person directly? Leave? Gently suggest the truth or an alternative way of framing things? Do I do the latter only if I am getting paid? And, if I object to a person's foolishness, what words and tone do I use? Measured speech? Respectful response? Scorn? Gentle and ironic humor? You might say, "Well, this all depends." And perhaps it does. But Proverbs then becomes the engine for thought, for us to reflect on our motives and actions and for us to decide on more effective ways to confront common occurrences. Thanks to people, there will never be an end to foolish examples on which we can practice our techniques.

THE KNOWABILITY OF THE HUMAN HEART

Can you really know and trust someone? It isn't just single people trying to find their mates that ask this question. It has been posed since time immemorial. Is the heart of another person really accessible to us? Can two souls become joined? Can we understand (and be understood) by someone else? People commit suicide because they don't think that anyone understands them. Thus, the question is of fairly significant import. I claim in my essays on the human heart below that Proverbs looks at this paradox (because the answer is "Yes and No") in at least four ways. It, as it were, takes the beautiful "diamond" of this most precious question and holds it up to different sources and intensities of light. How does Proverbs answer this question?

On the one hand, the human heart is unknowable. "The heart knows its own bitterness, and no stranger shares its joy," 14:10. We are, in our heart of hearts, isolated people. Lest we miss the point, Proverbs adds, three verses later, "Even in laughter the heart is sad, and the end of joy is grief," 14:13. We all return, after our brief appearance on life's stage, to our secret world of grief and sadness, where no one else can go. But, on the other hand, Proverbs expresses great hope for people to know each other's hearts. An initially cryptic proverb illustrates this: "Just as water reflects the face, so one human heart reflects another," 27:19. Yes, that is true, too, isn't it? We see our own reflection in the water, and so human hearts can be that reflective mirror to each other. We show each other who the other is; we are understood by the other.

Which will it be? Both, in fact. By posing the issue in the apparently unimposing framework of pithy statements, Proverbs encourages us to talk with others about knowing and being known; it teaches us to comb our autobiography for examples of people who have tried to know us (and perhaps succeeded); it gives us renewed energy to explore, without fear, this most vital question.

WISDOM: HUMAN ACHIEVEMENT OR DIVINE GIFT?

Is wisdom a human attainment or a divine gift? The immediate answer is "Both." But, if we take this question apart, we see that it begins to unfold for us like the peony, which is staggered by its own luxuriance. Wisdom has to be a divine gift, because it is so special and so basic to just and right functioning of the universe. Indeed, Proverbs affirms this: "The fear of the Lord is the beginning of wisdom," 9:10. Wisdom is God's counselor, the one who was there as a master worker when God was setting up the world, 8:30-31.

Yet, on the other hand, wisdom is very clearly a public or secular attainment, derived from experience and trial and error. Take any of dozens of examples. "To impose a fine on the innocent is not right, or to flog the noble for their integrity," 17:26. How does such a proverb develop? From years and years of patient observance of life. Flogging people for their integrity erodes the foundations of a community. You learn this because sometimes such people are flogged, and the entire community suffers. Or, more colorfully, "Better is a dry morsel with quiet than a house full of feasting with strife," 17:1. Perfectly said, isn't it? You can imagine people sitting around the city gate talking about their own or, more usually, others' domestic strife. Big parties. Loud feasts. Lots of quarrels. No good. Give me domestic harmony with a crust of bread rather than the life of the "rich and famous" with disharmony.

Wisdom is so highly prized in Proverbs because it is *both* a divine gift and a human attainment. Therein lies the invitation to consider wisdom and long for it.

IS THE PLANNED LIFE BETTER
THAN THE UNPLANNED LIFE?

This is another good question, to which Proverbs gives diverse answers. On the one hand, we are urged to make the most scrupulous plans, especially if it has to do with counseling the leaders of a nation. "Where there is no guidance, a nation falls, but in an abundance of counselors there is safety," 11:14. Or, "The plans of the diligent lead surely to abundance, but everyone who is hasty comes only to want," 21:5. Then, on the other hand, there is the realization that planning may really get you nowhere. "Do not boast about tomorrow, for you do not know what a day

7

may bring," 27: 1. Or, even more to the point, ""The human mind plans the way, but the Lord directs the steps," 16:9.

The reality of both of these emphases means that we need to think deeply about the role of planning in our lives. Several years ago, when I was pursuing a litigation attorney position, I was interviewed by a partner in a big law firm. He asked me where I wanted to be in "three to five years." Everything in the late 1990s seemed to be "three to five years." I think we unconsciously adopted recommendations from those involved in strategic planning, itself a sort of glitzy new field in those days, that we had to "think strategically" about our business. Thus, we ought, by extension, to think "strategically" about our lives. But if we do that too eagerly, we shut ourselves off to all kinds of interesting experiences, and we open ourselves to extreme disappointment, depression and worse if life doesn't work out the way that we "planned." Yet, on the other hand, I know that my days are most productive, in general, if I plan them.

Thus, the paradox. We plan our days but know we can't really plan our lives. Or, we try to plan our lives but realize that too much planning tends to lead to pain. What should it be? Proverbs helps us frame the question which leads to wisdom.

Proverbs explores many other difficult issues, such as, "How should the wise person present him/herself to the world?" and "What, ultimately, can you expect from life?" but you will have to read the following essays to see what it does with these. Suffice it to say that once you see the Book of Proverbs as presenting large life issues from a number of angles rather than simple, straightforward advice to young people on how to behave, you are ready to see it as a source of endless pleasure and instruction, a sort of engine for your own intellectual and practical life. Let's turn, for a moment, to some of the other pleasures that the Book of Proverbs provides.

ENTERING THE PLEASURE

The Book of Proverbs yields pleasure to us, among other things, through *gentle instruction, clever observation of life, inspirational and aspirational comment, and well-crafted statement.* Examples of each of these might be helpful. Take the *gentle instruction* in Proverbs 18: 13, 17.

> "If one gives answer before hearing,
>> it is folly and shame."
> "The one who first states a case seems right,
>> until the other comes and cross-examines."

Almost every proverb, and these are no exception, assumes a situation in life into which we, the reader, must imaginatively place ourselves. Here the situation assumed is where we are the recipients of information. We need to evaluate the truth of information that comes to us. Reports are always coming to us, from kids, from friends, from co-workers. We need to make a decision based on these reports. Someone makes a point, and it often seems to be right. We have a tendency to make snap judgments based on the report or even to express our opinion before the other can fully say his or her piece. But, we know from hard experience that v. 17 is true—a case often sounds convincing until different light is thrown upon it. So, the verse judges us and instructs us. It judges us because we know we have made hasty judgments in the past, that we haven't considered all relevant evidence, and that, as a result, our judgments have been flawed. It instructs us because it subtly teaches us to do better next time;

9

to make sure we truly have listened before making a judgment. Proverbs becomes the stimulus, then, for both theological and practical thought and action. I can, and I will, do better next time as I listen to those who make their cases to me. Gentle correction and instruction—what a pleasurable way to go!

An example of the *clever observation of life* is in 20:14. "'Bad, bad,' says the buyer, then goes away and boasts."

So brief, but so telling. Haven't we heard people tell us proudly how they managed to get a good deal on a purchase? One strategy to get a good deal is gently to denigrate the product or feign lack of interest in it. We figuratively say about the product, 'bad, bad,' even though we want it pretty badly. So, through our not seeming very interested, we think, the merchant will lower the price. He lowers it. We buy the goods. So delighted are we at our negotiating skill and cleverness with people that we go home and boast of it all in the hearing of any with ears. In the few words of this proverb, the Book of Proverbs isn't giving moral advice or theological judgment. It simply observes, in spare language, the way we live. The proverb captures the approach to "getting a good deal" that characterizes millions of people. It simply is a mirror of life, and we derive pleasure from seeing ourselves and others refracted in that mirror.

But Proverbs is also filled with *inspirational exhortations and aspirational statements*. It wants us to reach for the skies, so to speak, and to become better people. It wants us to become *wise* people. Proverbs is convinced that wisdom is the most valuable thing in the world and that getting it is much more important than securing gold and silver (3:14-15; 16:16). Wisdom is often predicated on a previous attitude of trust or fear of the Lord (1:7), but it makes big promises to those who adopt it. An example of the *inspirational and aspirational* nature of Proverbs is:

10

"The evil do not understand justice,

    but those who seek the Lord understand it

    completely." 28:5.

One might take this as an example of Proverbs' "overreaching" or promising more than it can deliver, but I think it is better to see the statement as encouraging us to pursue a certain kind of life, in this case the life of justice. You "seek the Lord" because by so doing you understand justice completely. Is the last phrase a hyperbole? Perhaps, or perhaps one can understand the last word (*kol* in Hebrew---"everything") to refer to understanding everything necessary about justice in the situation you find yourself. In this connection, Proverbs 28:5 is similar to the thought expressed in the great wisdom Psalm— Psalm 119. In language dripping with "wisdom" connotations, it says in Ps. 119: 98-99:

"Your commandment makes me wiser than my enemies,

    for it is always with me.

I have more understanding than all my teachers,

    for your decrees are my meditation,"

Something about seeking God, about pursuing the way of wisdom, about dedicating yourself to this life, leads to accomplishments that are somewhat counterintuitive—you understand more than your teachers. We understand all the justice about the situation that can be understood. Proverbs doesn't tell us precisely how these are true; it leaves the reflection to our imagination and it inspires us to pursue the path of justice- and wisdom-seeking. It *inspires* us to *aspire*.

11

Finally, the Book of Proverbs is filled with *well-crafted statements*. One could draw one's bow at a venture in Proverbs and hit such a statement on every page, but one such example is:

"There is gold, and abundance of costly stones;
    but the lips informed by knowledge are a
    precious jewel," 20:15.

Proverbs is replete with statements about the importance of good and well-formed words. But it isn't recommending this so that one can just have evidence in one's person of a finishing-school or university education. Proverbs has the audacity to claim that learning how and when to speak well is actually the key to one's success in life. "Words fitly spoken are like applies of gold in a setting of silver," 25:11. "To make an apt answer is a joy to anyone, and a word in season, how good it is!" 15:23. The indented proverb emphasizes the content of the words rather than their form, but it assures us that knowledge-driven speech is a most precious thing.

As a person who has led movements and hired and evaluated people, who has supervised dozens and has tried to help people think through their goals and ideas, I know that there is nothing more valuable than timely and well-expressed knowledge. Proverbs not only encourages us to pursue this knowledge but it gives us specific advice on how to do so. My aim in encouraging you to experience the pleasure of Proverbs is so that you will speak and act more wisely and do so with fuller and more accurate knowledge.

Sometimes we become so entranced by the beauty and potency of the Book of Proverbs that we think we become wise enough to speak the language of Proverbs, to make up proverbs on our own. I have tried to do some of this through my "Billphorisms" page on my web site. But, a later wisdom book, Sirach (13:26), gives us his impression of the difficulty of that:

> "The signs of a happy heart is a cheerful face,
> but to devise proverbs requires painful thinking,"

In this book I won't be making up many new proverbs. I will be satisfied, however, if we commit ourselves to understanding the paradoxes and pleasures of Proverbs and to becoming wise people in our day.

Chapter Two

AN INVITATION TO THE BOOK OF PROVERBS

SOMETIMES WE MISJUDGE PEOPLE. We meet them, aren't particularly impressed with them, and go away thinking that we won't have anything more to do with them. Then, something unexpected happens, and we see them in a new light. Upon looking at them a second time we discover all kinds of attractive features we didn't notice the first time around. Our first negative judgment clouded our ability to see what was truly before us.

Something similar happened to my friend from Chapter One when he learned that Proverbs was more than simply an advice manual for young people trying to find their way in life. When he began to see it as a book exploring nuance or paradox by presenting diverse proverbs that looked at a matter from different angles, he opened the book and, to his great surprise, saw the book anew. Individual proverbs began to leap off the page at him, filling him with insight, questions and even a laugh or two. He shook his head at me and said, "I wonder why I never saw these proverbs for so many years." My answer, "Because now you are looking at the Book of Proverbs through a different lens."

This chapter explores what my friend noticed when he began to see the Book of Proverbs differently. Then, it looks at the way the Book of Proverbs is organized, the styles of various proverbs and a few leading ideas of the book. Finally, lest we get carried away with how "relevant" the Book of Proverbs is, I close with mention of some proverbs I wouldn't touch "with a 10-foot pole."

SEEING THE BOOK OF PROVERBS DIFFERENTLY

Here are some of the proverbs that began to leap off the page at my friend, once he began to see the Book of Proverbs as a skillful exploration of nuance and paradox in life. I will make no comment on some of them; others, however, will stimulate some reflection. Let's begin with Prov. 26:17,

> "Like somebody who takes a passing dog by the ears
>   is one who meddles in the quarrel of another,"

Create the picture in your mind. No further comment is necessary. Or take Prov. 17:12,

> "Better to meet a she-bear robbed of its cubs
>   than to confront a fool immersed in folly."

I will discuss this in the context of how Proverbs says you should address the fool (see Day 13 below). Its message is not only clear; it immediately makes you smile. *'They* had fools, too,' we say.

"The rich is wise in self-esteem,
    but an intelligent poor person sees through
    the pose," 28:11.

A friend who formerly worked in a Midwestern city was hired by management of a large company to try to figure out why workers were discontented. After interviewing management and workers, my friend's report to management was, 'because they think you are living hypocritically. You do what you tell them not to do. You take long lunch breaks, you don't treat them well, you aren't consistent in discipline. This is their perception of you.' The "little people" saw through the "pose" of the "rich," who were convinced it was a worker problem. My friend was fired from his consulting position. The company no longer exists, though any connection between treatment of workers and failure of the company must have been completely coincidental.

"The lazy person says, 'There is a lion in the road!
    There is a lion in the streets!'" 26:13; 22: 13.

One of the categories of people whom Proverbs warns us against is the "sluggard" or "lazy" person. Such a person, for example, is so lazy that he lets his hand fall into the food dish only to be too tired to bring it to his mouth, 26:15. The proverb just quoted emphasizes something else about the lazy person—he uses convenient, even if unconvincing, excuses to keep him from getting out of bed and to work. "I can't work because there is danger out there!" A friend told me recently, only slightly in

17

jest, that a new excuse is starting to run throughout his circle of acquaintances. When a person doesn't want to do something, s/he blames the "recession." They can't come over for dinner because of the recession; they can't help do X because of the recession, etc. Indeed, a new blog began a few months ago, called the *Recessionista*, which contains helpful advice for those bogged down by the recession blues.[1]

> "Crush a fool in a mortar with a pestle along
> > with crushed grain,
> > but the folly will not be driven out," 27:22.

Proverbs, in general, doesn't believe that fools can rid themselves of their foolishness. Or, to put it differently, fools are incapable of taking discipline seriously. What a vivid picture this is to describe their utter inability to reform. Proverbs says it much better than we could. We usually say, "You just can't get through to him/her!" or "Boy is that person thick!" The image is powerful here because it suggests the very thing you would like to inflict on the fool—pulverizing him/her—is as futile as the expenditure of energy to do so would be.

> "With patience a ruler may be persuaded,
> > and a soft tongue can break bones," 25:15.

Near the end of the classic movie *Shawshank Redemption* Red, a wily old prisoner (Morgan Freeman), comments on Andy's (Tim Robbins) escape from Shawshank prison in Maine—an escape he had engineered by slowly cupping and carving away his cell wall until he hollowed out a space to escape. Red says,

---

1   http://therecessionista.blogspot.com/

"Geology is the study of pressure and time. That's all it takes, really. Pressure and time..." The verse just quoted from Proverbs reminds me of Red's line. A soft tongue breaks bones. What a view of the power of gentle persuasion. It not only is a statement brimming with hope, but it is said in such a terse, vivid and clear fashion that once you learn it, it can become stitched to your soul and become a central life value. Garrison Keillor once remarked that the orderly planning of Midwestern cities indicated that someone gave up lots of evenings for committee meetings; here we have lots of patience yielding completely counterintuitive results.

> "One who is slow to anger is better than the mighty,
>   and one whose temper is controlled than one
>   who captures a city," 16:32.

This proverb emphasizes the theme just broached but from a slightly different angle. That is what Prov. 25:15 teaches. Patience is essential in persuasion. But this proverb stresses the importance of controlling the temper. The major beneficiary of the controlled temper is the person tempted to anger. In brief compass Proverbs recognizes how difficult it is to control the emotion of anger; the one who does so ought to be featured in a triumph parade after a military victory. What also is noteworthy about this proverb is that the virtue encouraged ("slow to anger") is a characteristic shared by God. God is "slow to anger and abounding in steadfast love," Ex. 34:6. The wise person ultimately is an imitator of God, even as the wisdom s/he displays is most useful in the sphere of human relations.

> "Rash words are like sword thrusts,

but the tongue of the wise brings healing," 12:18

We can almost *feel* the intensity of this proverb. It can only have been written by those who have been slashed by the ugly, piercing, irresponsible sword of those who don't control the tongue. But the adversative in the proverb also is arresting. It emphasizes the healing power of the tongue for the wise. This verse provides not simply a description of life but a sort of exhortation to hone, develop, and cultivate the kind of tongue which heals. The tongue, with its "swordlike" shape, can be beaten into a plowshare of healing.

Many other striking individual proverbs could be introduced at this stage, but the point should be clear: once you are sympathetic to the philosophy I laid out in Chapter One—that the Book of Proverbs explores nuance in life—you are ready to see many of the individual proverbs as teaching valuable lessons in brief compass. By listening to, heeding, memorizing, recalling these and other proverbs, we are gradually committing ourselves to a new way of life—the way of wisdom. Unfolding that way will be one of the tasks of this book, though a preliminary description of the wise and the foolish will come in next chapter.

UNDERSTANDING THE FLOW OF PROVERBS

Most books on Proverbs begin with this section—i.e., a section which describes the type of literature Proverbs is, the various collections or proverbs that constitute the Book of Proverbs, and a few of its leading themes. A particular love of many scholars in the last generation has been to show "wisdom parallels" in antiquity—comparing the Book of Proverbs with wisdom from Egypt and Mesopotamia. Indeed, McKane's "new approach" to Proverbs in 1970 spent more than 200 pages "introducing" this comparative world of Proverbs.[2] Those who want to investigate that further are urged to pick up his book. My concern in this section is to say enough about the flow and rhythm of Proverbs so that you can profitably read and study this ancient classic.

The Book of Proverbs as it comes down to us is of uncertain date. It was, along with Ecclesiastes and Song of Solomon, ascribed to King Solomon (10th century BCE), but even sections of Proverbs state quite clearly that they were composed or compiled by others (see 25:1; 30:1; 31:1). We don't know, then, when the book reached its final form. Nor do we know the precise place in the life of ancient Israel where this book would have been most used. Is the "assumed world" of Proverbs the world of the royal court? Chapter 16 would support that assumption. But lots of the instruction reads as if it is a sort of "family manual," with the emphasis being on instruction from parent to child on how to live well in the society. Then, some might argue that it found its natural home in a "school" or "scribal" world, though the shape or even existence of these schools is far from evident. Thus, rather than spending a lot of time hypothesizing over many things that exist only in scholars' imaginations, I will move to the structure of the book.

Most would agree that the Book of Proverbs consists of seven smaller collections of proverbs. Those sections are:

> 1:1-9:18 General Wisdom Exhortations
> 10:1-22:16 Individual Solomonic Proverbs
> 22:17-24:22 Thirty Sayings of the Wise

---

2   William McKane, *Proverbs: A New Approach* (Westminster, 1970).

When most people think of biblical proverbs, they think of those in collections 2-7. Collection 1, however, is different. Instead of short, pithy aphorisms, collection 1 consists of longer sermons or lectures on the pursuit of wisdom, the dangers of loose women and the avoidance of certain types of people (the sluggard, for example). Collections 2 and 5 are the "Solomonic" proverbs which are so familiar to us, with either synonymous or antithetical parallelism of its two cola (each line of the proverb is referred to as a colon), with lots of emphasis on the wise and the foolish. Nuance and paradox, as well as humor and startling observations, come out of these proverbs and make them a continual source of learning. Collections 3 and 4 are much briefer, most similar to Egyptian parallels, and are concerned in general with the same subjects as the Solomonic proverbs. Sometimes, however, an individual proverb in these collections stretches on for several verses. Finally, collections 6 and 7 are attributed to two unknown individuals, Agur and Lemuel. Proverbs 30 specializes in proverbs of the "threes and fours,"[3] while the signature element of Proverbs 31 is the description of the capable wife (31:10-31). An example of the "threes and fours" shows you what I mean (30:15-16):

"Three things are never satisfied;

four never say, 'Enough':

_____

3 An example is in vv. 18-19, "Three things are too wonderful for me; four I do not understand: the way of an eagle in the sky, the way of a snake on a rock, the way of a ship on the high seas, and the way of a man with a girl."

Sheol, the barren womb,

> the earth ever thirsty for water,
>
> and the fire that never says, 'Enough.'"

While all portions of the Book of Proverbs will come in for extensive comment in this book, I am most interested in those single, seemingly solitary and isolated, proverbs from 10:1 until the end of the book. I will often double back to pick up insights from Proverbs 1-9, but my focus will be on delineating the way of wisdom as it is found in collections 2-7 and especially in 2-5.

In the chapters in collections 2-5 (chapters 10-29), we have just under 600 verses. In those 600 verses are perhaps 450 proverbs. There are, for example, many multi-verse single proverbs, such as in 24:30-34 or 23:29-35. Then, of the perhaps 450 proverbs that remain, about 50 either repeat themselves or have significant textual problems. Examples are the nearly identical four proverbs on the importance of having just scales or balances (11:1; 16:11; 20:10, 23) or the two on the sluggard (26:13; 22:13). Of the remaining 400 or so proverbs in this section, about 250 are discussed or mentioned in this book. I don't do justice to all the proverbs about riches and poverty; nor do I talk in detail of the proverbs relating to the king. Yet, I try to give a detailed and thorough-enough consideration to those 250 so that the central nuances/paradoxes and message of Proverbs are clear.

Before moving to the final section of this chapter, I add a word about themes of the Book of Proverbs. It might be helpful to mention, in the first instance, what is *absent*, rather than what is present, in Proverbs. The word *qadosh*, the standard biblical word for "holy", is absent. This is significant because "holy" is normally used elsewhere in the Bible to describe the kind of life one should live, and Proverbs is all about right living. There is very little about good family life, marriage or even friendship, even though the book focuses on success in personal relationships. Nothing is mentioned on how you should face death properly. Instead of the vocabulary of holiness or purity or sacrifice or covenant or family life, however, Proverbs picks up on another word (abomination), and uses it to divide the world between the wise and foolish, the wicked and righteous. I find the vocabulary of wisdom and foolishness to be of great value for today. Yet the language of wisdom and foolishness itself opens a nuanced world, for we also find other people hanging out with the wise and foolish, such as the simple, lazy, mocker, and others. The next chapter will delineate the people you meet in Proverbs. The essence of the Book of Proverbs, unfolded in the next chapter, is that Proverbs believes that pursuing wisdom can lead to mastery over the process of living—which is not a bad definition of the idea of wisdom. It is a very strong claim, and the examination of this claim is at the heart of this book, beginning in the next chapter.

PROVERBS I WOULDN'T TOUCH
WITH A TEN-FOOT POLE

I have deovted so much attention trying to make the case for why one should study Proverbs that one might get the impression that it is a book written directly to our situation in the 21st century. Yet, it bears signs of the world that created it, and this section lists some proverbs which, frankly, just don't seem to resonate that well with our world. See what you think.

First are a series of proverbs about a contentious wife. A few examples are Prov. 21:9, 19.

"It is better to live in a corner of the housetop than
in a house shared with a contentious wife."

"It is better to live in a desert land than with a
contentious and fretful wife."

Some modern translations try to change the operative word here to "spouse," but that isn't what the text says. I suppose in fact the proverb is probably true, but in our day we would probably wish there was greater balance. "Better to live in a corner of a housetop than with an angry man..." We like equal or even-handed treatment in the 21st century. Proverbs didn't feel constrained by our constraints. A similar proverb is 27:15-16.

Then there are the proverbs on physical punishment. Some might not find the following problematic:

"Those who spare the rod hate their children,
but those who love them are diligent to
discipline them," 13:24.

But look at 23:13:

"Do not withhold discipline from your children;
if you beat them with a rod, they will not die."

Regardless of what you might think about the proper way to discipline a child, I think that 23:13 is problematic. In fact, children do die from beatings. We haven't just learned that in the past 40 years, but this reality has been one of the reasons behind campaigns to end child abuse. Some might respond, 'well, the wise person knows how to discipline the child and will realize that it will only be conducted in a moderate fashion,' but even that statement ignores the great emphasis on Proverbs on the prevalence of the fool in human life. Fools might not be expected to discipline wisely; indeed, they do nothing wisely. Why give them an excuse for beating, when they will no doubt do that foolishly also? Another problematic proverb on punishment is in 20:30,

> "Blows that wound cleanse away evil;
>> beatings make clean the innermost parts."

I have to confess that the motivation to "cleanse" a person through beating them may be fraught with more difficulties than benefits...

There are a series of proverbs that seemingly are just observations of life, though many commentators read them with a moral/istic view. What would you do with these?

> "A bribe is like a magic stone in the eyes of those
>> who give it;
>> wherever they turn they prosper," 17:8.

Is the author condemning this practice; simply observing the effectiveness of bribes; commending it? On a similar note we have in 21:14,

> "A gift in secret averts anger;
>> and a concealed bribe in the bosom, strong wrath,"

It almost seems to be commending the latter as a way to win favor with important people. How about this one?

"Gray hair is a crown of glory;
   it is gained in a righteous life," 16:31.

Maybe, but often not. In fact, the day before I wrote these words, an 88 year-old man burst into the Holocaust Museum on the National Capitol Mall, killing a security guard. Apparently he had been "enraged" for years. His gray hair was no crown of glory. Countless other examples of gray hair not being a sign of either wisdom or righteousness are ready at hand. Indeed, there is no sadder sight than an old fool. Much better, in my judgment, is 20:29,

"The glory of youths is their strength,
   but the beauty of the aged is their gray hair."

The latter emphasizes a glory attendant upon each age; the earlier proverb states something that is often not true. Then, do you believe the following?

"Truthful lips endure forever,
   but a lying tongue lasts only a moment," 12:19.

This may express the confidence that truth will eventually win out, but it doesn't say that. It says that lying tongues last for only a moment. Maybe in God's time, if a thousand years are like a day, this is true. But if one has to resort to such interpretive gymnastics, it is as if you are too embarrassed to face the verse head-on.

Let's conclude with this seemingly innocuous proverb:

"No harm happens to the righteous,
 but the wicked are filled with trouble," 12:21.

No comment is necessary, but I wonder how many people of faith would affirm that statement without equivocation?

CONCLUSION

Lest we forget it, Proverbs is about the people you meet in the world and the way you conduct yourself to be wise. Let's turn now to the final introductory chapter, which considers these two subjects in greater detail.

Chapter Three:

THE PEOPLE YOU'LL MEET[1] AND THE PLACES YOU'LL GO[2]

THIS FINAL INTRODUCTORY CHAPTER focuses on the life of wisdom or, alternatively said, how one lives wisely in the world. Much more will be said about this as the next 31 min-chapters unfold, but it is useful to suggest an overview of the "way of wisdom" and its features here. Three issues will occupy me in this chapter: a Biblical definition of wisdom; a description of the types of people you meet in the world, according to Proverbs; and a presentation of the image or root metaphor of life, according to Proverbs.

From the three introductory chapters of this book, then,

---

1 This isn't the title of a Dr. Seuss book, but is the name of a song sung by the Cat in the Hat and Mrs. Buttons about the people that Jeremy Jalloo will meet in life. This song appeared in the Nickelodeon (TV channel) show entitled the *Wubbulous World of Dr. Seuss*, which premiered late in 1996.

2 The 1990 book by Dr. Seuss is called "Oh, the Places You'll Go."

I am trying to present wisdom in Proverbs as a complex and alluring subject that is, at the same time, intellectually gripping and practically enticing. Wisdom calls us to "turn in here" (9:4) today, and this chapter tells you what that simple invitation means.

DEFINING WISDOM

In a word, Biblical wisdom may be defined as life-mastery. Proverbs believes that life can, to a great extent, be learned or mastered. There are certain "rules" of life that, if internalized, can lead you to "riches and honor and life" (22:4). But this kind of wisdom doesn't come overnight, nor is it easily accessible. It is the product of discipline, and discipline is a process of mastering principles, being corrected and rebuked (and sometimes being "spanked"), and finally putting into practice a series of very practical principles in life. The following 31 chapters/essays exposit those principles. Here, however, I need to say more about the Biblical idea of wisdom.

The word *hakam/hokmah*, translated "wise person" and "wisdom," appears hundreds of times in the Bible, but the clearest illustration of its meaning in Proverbs comes from passages outside of Proverbs: Exodus 31 and 36 and Ecclesiastes 8. In the former passage, the Lord spoke to Moses about the construction of the Tabernacle in the wilderness. God had equipped certain people with the skill to make the Tabernacle; Moses is to make use of them. The specific words are important:

"The Lord spoke to Moses: See, I have called by
name Bezalel son of Uri son of Hur, of the tribe of
Judah: and I have filled him with the divine spirit,

with ability, intelligence, and knowledge in every kind of craft, to devise artistic designs...," Ex. 31: 1-4; similar language is also used in Ex. 36:1-2.

The word translated "ability" here is *hokmah*. That is, God has equipped Bezalel with the ability or wisdom to complete the hard task of building the Tabernacle. The words translated "intelligence" and "knowledge" are also highly freighted words in the Book of Proverbs, but the focus here is on *hakam/hokmah*. *Hokmah* is therefore the mastery of a skill that enables one to do a job well. Bezalel worked well in gold, silver and bronze; he was "wise" in those areas. The wise person, thus, has a competence, a skill, a mastery of something.

The important question following from this is, "What is the scope of the wise *person's* competence?" If the wise builder has skill to do his/her work in construction and the wise farmer would be knowledgeable of all things agronomic and the wise shopkeeper knows all the lore of keeping store, what is the scope of the wise *person's* competence? Ecclesiastes 8:1 is helpful in answering this question.

"Who is like the wise man?
    And who knows the interpretation of a thing?
Wisdom makes one's face shine,
    And the hardness of one's countenance is changed."

This verse gives us more than we anticipated. It not only answers our question on the scope of the wise person's competence but it tells us that there are attractive physiognomic consequences of being wise—it makes our faces "shine." In 2010 terms, I think it makes one look "alert."

But the interesting point for me is in the first part of the verse just quoted. The wise person has skill, to be sure, and it is in the "interpretation of a thing." A wise person is a hermeneut[3], an interpreter, a person who knows what things mean, a person who can give, as we say, the "lay of the land," the situation "in a nutshell," the scope of a problem, the nature of its reality. This interpretive capacity lies at the heart of Biblical wisdom.

Does this mean that the wise person knows it all? Of course not. But what it *does* mean is that the wise person loves knowledge and its acquisition, and that s/he looks to the cultivation of knowledge as the fuel for developing the interpretive capacity so that, in the end, one leads a wise life. As Proverbs tells us, "An intelligent mind acquires knowledge, and the ear of the wise seeks knowledge," 18:15.

Biblical wisdom is the kind of skill that can find its home in a variety of work and life contexts. I can easily imagine a wise capitalist (just as I can think of a foolish one) or a wise sensualist (if by that term we mean a person overwhelmed by the sensual richness of life). A wise person need not be in the academic world; indeed, wise people are probably as rare in academia as they are in any other profession. I have met wise horticulturalists who know how the meaning of plants can help interpret the life of humans. On the other hand, I have also met fairly foolish and even stupid or insensate politicians and academicians, who are supposed to have wisdom in order to do their work well.

Thus, Biblical wisdom is available to all but, as we will find,

---

3   I am almost coining the word here. The Oxford English Dictionary has an entry under "hermeneut," which it calls "rare," and which it defines as "an interpreter; esp. one of those employed in the early Church to interpret the service to worshippers who used a different language." The OED says that this term only entered the English language in 1965. I am using the term in the broader sense of "interpreter of life."

it is embraced by few. Wisdom doesn't easily compete with the "noise" of the culture around us. Money or pleasure or political power hold themselves out in a much more alluring way than wisdom. But wisdom is there, gently calling us. It is recognized and embraced by those who seek some kind of mastery of life. It is the pearl of great price, the most valuable thing in the world. This book lays out how you can make the life of wisdom central to your own life.

THE PEOPLE YOU'LL MEET IN PROVERBS

The Book of Proverbs is an intellectually demanding book because it requires us to think of how a pithy statement of ten words or so might be true. It is also practically demanding because it is alive to the people and situations we encounter in life, and it suggests how we should act in these situations. Several types of people make up the universe of Proverbs. A complete taxonomy of the people in Proverbs' world isn't possible because sometimes it is difficult to know whether Proverbs is trying to introduce us to a "type" of person or just a characteristic of the wise or foolish person. For example, there are several proverbs relating to the "clever" (*arum*) person (22:3; 27:12). One is:

> "The clever see danger and hide;
>   but the simple go on, and suffer for it."

Are the clever another "type" of person? I don't think so, and I will classify them with the "wise." Or, on the other hand, Proverbs sometimes talks about the "hothead":

> "One given to anger stirs up strife,

33

and the hothead causes much transgression," 29:22.

Is the "hothead" a "type" of person? I don't think so. I think s/he belongs with the fool. Like various species of a plant genus, so the "hothead" or the "clueless" belong to the genus of "fool."

Yet there are categories of people beyond just the wise and the foolish. Proverbs has a complex moral universe, and the people that constitute it are themselves quite various. I will briefly introduce six types of people here. From "best" to "worst" they are: (1) the "more wise"; (2) the wise; (3) the simple or gullible; (4) the fool; (5) the sluggard or lazy person; and (6) the mocker or scoffer. Proverbs also spends a lot of time distinguishing between the just and unjust, the good and the wicked, but it often overlays these words on the six categories just mentioned without specifying anything more about how these relate to each other.

Thus, the task here is to say a word about these six categories of people. We will meet them all in much more detail in the following essays. The "more wise" is an important category because it stresses that the Book of Proverbs is aware that you can *grow* in wisdom. We have these people introduced in the preface:

"Let the wise also hear and gain in learning,
    and the discerning acquire skill," 1:5.

Indeed, statements such as "whoever loves discipline loves knowledge" (12:1) are only comprehensible in a universe where the wise are those who grow, mature and become better interpreters and masters of life.

The second group is the wise. The category of "wise"

34

includes the shrewd, the righteous and the prudent, and thus whatever is attributed to the latter will be vested in the wise. I will patiently unfold his/her characteristics in the following chapters, but the essence of wisdom is a willingness and ability to *pause and ponder* rather than to react immediately and unthinkingly to the cycle of meaningless life all around us (15:28).

> "The mind of the righteous ponders how to answer
>   but the mouth of the wicked pours out evil."

Once you leave the category of the wise, however, you don't immediately fall in with fools. A good number of people fit into a third category: the gullible or simple. These are inexperienced people. We normally think of an inexperienced person as young, but anyone can be inexperienced, as long as the area is "new" to them. Indeed, Proverbs even holds out for the possibility of there being wise children (13:1); not all young people are simple. There is a bit of the "simple" in each of us. The major issue for the simple is the dangers they face—dangers of which they are unaware. The danger is not that they will immediately be swallowed up by lions, tigers and bears but that they will fall into a life of foolishness. The simple just don't have enough experience or insight into aspects of life to make wise decisions. They need lots of instruction, correction and rebuke in order not to fall into foolishness.

> "The simple believe everything,
>   but the clever consider their steps," 14:15.

The task of the wise is to make sure that the simple don't fall into foolishness. It is a tall order.

The fool appears to be the largest generic category in Proverbs. Abraham Lincoln said that God must love the "common man" because He made so many of them; the Book of Proverbs is probably amazed, though it never says so, at how many people in God's good creation have ended up becoming fools. The fool will receive his/her due in the following pages, but a central characteristic of the fool is inability to listen and consider another person's ideas:

"A fool takes no pleasure in understanding,
    but only in expressing personal opinion," 18:2.

What most pleases a fool is listening to him/herself. A fool is staggered by his own brilliance, amazed by her own attractiveness. A fool is hasty in speech. A helpful contrast to the wise/prudent is expressed in 12:16,

"Fools show their anger at once,
    but the prudent ignore an insult."

Fools are *immediateists*. Reaction to the world takes place *right now*.

The world of fools is richly populated, according to Proverbs. While there really are only two categories of "the wise," there are three of fools. The other two are the lazy/sluggard and the mocker/scoffer. Both of these are fools because they don't interpret life well and they react without due consideration. Yet they also have other unattractive characteristics. The lazy, to befit his name, just can't get out of bed. He is possessed by unrealistic and unhelpful fears, and thus never ventures out of his house.

"The lazy person says, 'There is a lion outside!
I shall be killed in the streets!'" 22:13.

Proverbs never probes the psychological world of the sluggard (i.e., what *makes* the person a sluggard); it does make the distinction, however, between the poor who are sluggards, and do not deserve help, and the poor who are poor who invite our solicitude.

Finally, there is the scoffer or mocker. The scoffer is the most dangerous person in Proverbs because s/he is a community destroyer. Proverbs has many names for this person: the "perverse" (16:28), the "violent" (16:29), or the "scoundrel" (16:27), but it is the same person behind all these nomenclative designations. Such a person is so dangerous because ultimately s/he is interested only in self and not the good of the community. The root problem of the scoffer is arrogance or "arrogant pride" (21:24). The entire universe consists of a circle which only the mocker can occupy. These people really do exist in the world—in frighteningly large numbers. It doesn't take many of them to wreck the work of the wise. It is this "problem" that led to the writing of Ecclesiastes..but *that* book is beyond the scope of *this* book.

THE WAY YOU'LL GO IN THE BOOK OF PROVERBS

The root metaphor in Proverbs for living in accordance with wisdom is to "follow the way" or to "keep to the path." Wisdom is conceived of as a way or path, straight rather than crooked, along which one travels. I will say more about this way in a moment, but it might first be good to ruminate on alternative pictures of the religious life so that Proverbs' "way" takes on a more compelling cast.

Three other pictures of the religious life, grounded in the Scriptures but developed in literature and music, are the religious life as journey, as battle and as race. The journey motif has especially been emphasized in recent days, with a leading expression of it found in W.H. Auden's *Christmas Oratorio*:

"He is the Way.
Follow Him through the Land of Unlikeness;
You will see rare beasts, and have unique
    adventures.

He is the Truth.
Seek Him in the Kingdom of Anxiety;
You will come to a great city that has expected your
    return for years.

He is the Life.
Love Him in the World of the Flesh;
And at your marriage all its occasions shall dance
    for joy."[4]

While the journey motif resonates powerfully with us today, the "life as race" metaphor has an ancient origin—the Epistle to the Hebrews (12:1-2):

"Therefore, since we are surrounded by so great a
cloud of witnesses, let us also lay aside every weight
and the sin that clings so closely, and let us run with
perseverance the race that is set before us, looking to

4   Part IV: Chorus. Text is here: http://hopeeternal.wordpress.com/2008/01/08/
christmas-oratorio-w-h-auden/

Jesus the pioneer and perfecter of our faith, who for the sake of the joy that was set before him endured the cross, disregarding its shame, and has taken his seat at the right hand of the throne of God."

Finally, the picture of the Christian life as battle is derived from the Scriptures (e.g., II. Tim. 2:3), but finds its most vivid instantiation in the life of the desert hermits of the ancient world as well as some hymns of modern Christendom. We all know the 1865 hymn of Sabine Baring-Gould:

"Onward Christian soldiers marching as to war, with the cross of Jesus going on before..."

Or, from "This is My Father's World":

"This is my Father's world. The battle is not
    done.
Jesus who died will be satisfied, and earth and
    heaven be one."

Thus, Proverbs' image of the life of faith as keeping to the way or walking in the straight path is only one of many images of life we might adopt. It is, however, a useful and powerful one. Its virtue is its recognition that the main dangers we face in life are distractions and false allures rather than a lurking Devil or a sin nature that has to be subdued. A few verses from Proverbs will illustrate its emphasis:

"Trust in the Lord with all your heart,
    and do not rely on your own insight.

In all your ways acknowledge him,
        And he will make straight your paths," 3:5-6.

"I have taught you the way of wisdom;
    I have led you in the paths of the upright.
When you walk, your step will not be hampered;
    And if you run, you will not stumble," 4:11-12.

"Put away from you crooked speech,
        and put devious talk far from you.
Let your eyes look directly forward,
        And your gaze be straight before you.
Keep straight the path of your feet,
        And all your ways will be sure.
Do not swerve to the right or to the left;
        Turn your foot away from evil," 4:24-27.

The "way" or "path" keeps popping up as we move to other sections of Proverbs, though sometimes in slightly different words:

"It is the wisdom of the clever to understand where
        they go," 14:8.

"The simple believe everything,
        but the clever consider their steps," 14:15.

"Folly is a joy to one who has no sense,
        but a person of understanding walks straight
        ahead," 15:21.

UNDERSTANDING THE WAY

According to Proverbs one just doesn't alight on the way as from a horse or carriage and begin one's path in life. There are two preliminary steps for the one who will walk "straight ahead." First s/he needs to know what it is to be humbled. Then, s/he has to understand the fear of the Lord (1:7). A word on each will complete the chapter.

Proverbs is aware that one of the most pernicious snares in life is pride. "Pride goes before destruction and a haughty spirit before a fall," 16:18. The mocker manifests pride (21:24), and the fool tends to be "wise in his own eyes," 26:12. Learning the way of humility is a sort of divine antidote to pride. Like Zora Neale Hurston, who had "been in Sorrow's kitchen and licked out all the pots," the person who aspires to wisdom must first be acquainted with lessons in humility. The Hebrew word for humility comes from the verb "to be oppressed" or "to be bent." Thus, the concept of humility arises from the common human experience of being treated unjustly. In such a situation we feel dishonored, even humiliated. All things taste bad; we bear as if it were a heavy weight of sorrow and discomfort. We know that we are dust and to dust we shall return. Going through this kind of experience of oppression or "being bent" is the first step in Biblical humility. We learn that we are common clay, but then we rebel against the unjust treatment, and we vow never to let it happen again. W cannot forget the pain, however, and we know that if we ever accomplish anything in life it will not be despite the humiliation but, in all likelihood, because of it. It has become our spur to accomplishment and to a better life.

The Scriptures focus deeply on the experience of being bent or being oppressed and its formative influence in making us humble people.

"It was good for me that I was humbled,
    so that I might learn your statutes," Psalm 119:71.

"It is good for one to bear the yoke in youth,
    to sit alone in silence when the Lord has imposed it,
to put one's mouth to the dust (there may yet be
        hope),
to give one's cheek to the smiter, and be filled with
        insults," Lamentations 3:27-30.

And who can read the last verses without thinking immediately about the humiliation suffered by the Servant of God in Isaiah 53, a passage through which the New Testament interprets the life and death of Jesus?

Proverbs is clear on the matter. In order to get to honor, one must first experience humility.

"Toward the scorners he is scornful,
    but to the humble he shows favor," 3:34.

"Before destruction one's heart is haughty,
    but humility goes before honor," 18:12.

"The fear of the Lord is instruction in wisdom,
    and humility goes before honor," 15:33.

This last verse triggers the other thing a person on the way of wisdom has to learn, according to Proverbs. It is the fear of the Lord. The fear of the Lord is said to be the beginning of both knowledge (1:7) and wisdom (9:10). Prof. Bruce Waltke says that the Biblical concept of "fear of the Lord" has both rational and nonrational aspects.[5] The "rational" aspect is the revelation of God, also called the law or statutes of God. Thus, the "fear of the Lord" can simply be the divine "rules" of the life of faith. Its nonrational aspect, however, is more to the point here. It suggests an "emotional response of fear, love and trust." The two polar reactions, of fear and love, of terror and trust, are not incompatible. According to the Scriptures, one both stands in awe of and loves God. That, in a nutshell, is the fear of God.[6]

CONCLUSION

Embarking and staying on the way of wisdom is probably the most important decision one makes in life. Distractions abound. One might even complain that this "way" sounds more like a straightjacket than a way of freedom. But those who have decided to commit themselves to the way of wisdom find in it a tremendous sense of freedom, power and direction. The next 31 mini-essays/chapters will describe that way.

---

5   *The Book of Proverbs, 1-15*, pp. 100-101.

6   I write more about the idea of the "fear of God" in an essay published on my website, which examines the story of David and Bathsheba. http;//www.drbilllong.com/LectionaryIV/IISam12II.html

Part Two

The Life of Wisdom

Yearning for Wisdom

Day One

PROVERBS 30:24-28; LEARNING WISDOM FROM THE ANIMALS

24 "Four things on earth are small,
   yet they are exceedingly wise:
25 the ants are a people without strength,
   yet they provide their food in the summer;
26 the badgers are a people without power,
   yet they make their homes in the rocks;
27 the locusts have no king,
   yet all of them march in rank;
28 the lizard can be grasped in the hand,
   yet it is found in kings' palaces."

THE BOOK OF PROVERBS is about teaching and learning. We learn by example, by discipline, by revelation, by mastery of specific principles. Indeed, so much emphasis is placed in Proverbs on the importance of wisdom for living that we might get the impression that wisdom is exclusively the possession of or domain of humans. But this text, which begins our expositions of Proverbs, teaches otherwise. Wisdom is found in the small and vulnerable animals. What is interesting is that these animals act wisely seemingly by *instinct*, whereas humans must utilize a variety of methods to learn wisdom. What the animals do effortlessly and perfectly, we humans strive for intermittently and unskillfully. Humans must study wisdom, store it up and then make use of proverbs in right times and circumstances to aid in the mastery of life (cf. Prov. 22:18), while the animals display it by nature. Who, really, are the "lords" of creation?

The realization that animals display wisdom ought to teach us humility and spur our inquisitiveness. As will be shown in later essays, humility is one of the cornerstone values of Proverbs. "Toward the scorners he (God) is scornful, but to the humble he shows favor," 3:34. "When pride comes, then comes disgrace; but wisdom is with the humble," 11:2. In addition, these verses stimulate our inquisitiveness to look to the natural world for other lessons of wisdom. If animals can be examples of wisdom, may plants? Can we learn something from studying the blooming patterns of flowers? Our promotional systems in colleges and universities (tenure) is built on the notion that you have to show your promise very early in your career to have lifetime connection with a school. What if, however, a person is more like an aster, blooming late in summer, than a lilac, which first appears with "ever-returning spring"?[1] Again, if trees might have "standing" in a legal sense, according to former US Supreme Court Justice William O. Douglas, might they also teach wisdom?[2]

---

1   From Walt Whitman's moving 1865 tribute to the memory of Abraham Lincoln, "When Lilacs last in the Dooryard Bloom'd."

2   Douglas asked this whimsical, and rather wild, question in a dissent in *Sierra Club v. Morton*, 405 US 727 (1972). Actually, as things have developed,

In the verses just quoted, the wisdom of the animals is presented in a series of contrasts. The animal is first introduced in its vulnerability and smallness; then the compensatory wisdom is related. Since no human has ever trained a locust or guided an ant to collect food in summer, this wisdom must either be providential or instinctual. The ant shows wisdom in its provision of *sustenance*; the badgers show it through making *shelters*; the locusts are noteworthy because of their *strength* when gathered together; the lizard enjoys the *spaciousness* of the king's palace. The Psalmist could say, after surveying the vast works of creation: "O Lord, how manifold are your works! In wisdom you have made them all. The earth is full of your creatures" (Psalm 104:24), and Proverbs would agree with that assessment. Let's look in a little more depth at the wisdom of the creatures.

THE ANT, THE ROCK BADGER, THE LOCUST, THE LIZARD

Our verses appear amid a collection of "threes and fours" that characterize Proverbs 30. Some groupings of threes or four in this chapter are "too wonderful" for the author (vv. 18-19); others make the world unendurable (vv. 21-23). In this case we have four things that are small but exceedingly wise. Their wisdom enables them to survive and flourish despite their vulnerability and individual weakness. The phrase "exceedingly wise" (v. 24) translates a rare Hebrew phrase, which is literally "the wisest of those with wisdom." The author doesn't seem to be saying that these animals are the wisest of the other (non-human) animals. his seemingly "off-the-wall" question has fueled a lot of passion in the environmental community regarding protecting the "rights" of living things in nature.

49

The message is that these insects and animals are the wisest of all living creatures. Take that, O Human!

The ant plays a larger role in Proverbs than some categories of humans. "Go to the ant, you lazybones" (old translation—"you sluggard"); consider its ways and be wise," 6:6. The ant is our teacher of wisdom. It instructs in food preparation, in planning, in how to get things done without a leader (6:7-8). The ant "prepares its food in summer, and gathers its sustenance in harvest," 6:8. In so doing, the ant exceeds the capacity of the sluggard, the simple child and the fool. Note Prov. 10:5,

> "A child who gathers in summer is prudent,
>> but a child who sleeps in harvest brings shame,"

> "Those who till their land will have plenty of food,
>> but those who follow worthless pursuits have no
>> sense," Prov. 12:11.

A basic principle of Pauline theology is that we ought to pursue the *imitatio Christi*, the imitation of Christ. The author of Proverbs might, tongue in check, suggest something else: the centrality of the *imitatio formicarum*.

There is some scholarly disagreement about which animal is meant by the *shaphan*, usually translated "rock badger" or "coney" or "hyrax." Waltke, among others, argues that this is the *Procavia syriacus*.[3] It is small (about the size of a rabbit), with tiny ears and dense fur. It neither has numerical or physical strength. Thus, it has to survive by its wits—which it does by dwelling in the rocks. No doubt the life patterns of the rock badger became legendary in Israel. You wonder if it became the sort of envy of

---

3   Waltke, op. cit., vol. 2, p. 497.

people, just as the cat is sometimes the envy of despairing people today. "Look at the cat, seemingly oblivious to all problems. And here I suffer." To those who have the tendency to muse, as the sages of Israel did, the problem of the rock badger was no doubt an a-musing pastime. "Look at that creature. So small, so unprotected. Look at our politicians. So seemingly invulnerable and powerful. The rock badgers survive quite nicely. Our strong politicians fall. Learn wisdom from those furry creatures."

A different picture confronts us when we think of the wisdom of locusts. Locusts are the bane of Middle Eastern societies, and their predacious instincts and edacious character are often noted in biblical literature.

> "What the cutting locust has left,
>   the swarming locus has eaten.
> What the swarming locus has left,
>   the hopping locust has eaten,
> and what the hopping locust has left,
>   the destroying locust has eaten," Joel 1:4.

Proverbs here (v. 27) notes their unity or, in the literal language of the verse, how they are "divided" (in ranks, such as an invading army). Their "wisdom" consists in an ability to organize and wreak untold devastation *without a king*. When there was no king in Israel, and everyone did what was right in his own eyes (Jud. 21:25), there was chaos. Human beings need ordered societies, but even in 2010 we know that many of those ordered societies don't assure the rights of subjects. When millions of Chinese organized for opening ceremonies of the 2008 Summer Olympics, which were pulled off without a hitch, one Chinese leader was quoted as saying, 'well, we might have done this to

51

the admiration of the world, but we are nothing compared to the North Koreans. They are the world's best organizers." Ironies abound, even as we note the wisdom of the locust.

Finally, the lizards are wise because, despite their vulnerability (they can be caught in the hand), they live in the king's palace. People in Proverbs only have access to the king if they have a most attractive confluence of personal features. Indeed, unless you act properly, you should fear for your life in the presence of a king:

> "When you sit down to eat with a ruler,
>   observe carefully what is before you,
> and put a knife to your throat
>   if you have a big appetite," 23:1-2.

> "Those who love a pure heart and are gracious in
>   speech will have the king as a friend," 22:11.

But the lizard seemingly has no concern for this. It just slithers into the king's palace and takes up residence there. Some commentators remark that these vulnerable creatures aren't wiped out by kings because they are useful—they eat smaller bugs.

Wisdom and its lessons are all around us. But, before we turn to a book to learn the lessons of wisdom, we ought take a look around. Wisdom may be crawling, hanging, darting, plunging, or growing nearby.

Day Two

PROVERBS 16:16 AND THE CENTRAL IMPORTANCE OF WISDOM

"How much better to get wisdom than gold!
To get understanding is to be chosen rather than
silver," 16:16.

OUR FIRST AND NATURAL REACTION to this verse is to acknowledge its truth in public but then, in private, burst out laughing. Wisdom better than gold? Understanding to be preferred to silver? We laugh to ourselves because we basically don't believe this verse is true. Or, better said, we don't live as if it is true. We spend far more time getting gold, and worrying about gold, than attaining wisdom. If we were given a choice between the two, most people would, without question, choose the money, and preferably in a lump-sum payout. But here is the verse in all its simplicity, telling us that wisdom is better than gold and understanding than silver. Surely this is an expression of the philosophy of the "wisdom movement" of ancient Israel, as scholars would frame it, but is it true? Does it make any sense in the world of the 21st century? Let me put it this way: *if* the verse is true, and if we conclude it is true *for us*, then we may have some pretty radical reorienting of our lives to do. *If* it is true, the pursuit of wisdom has to be placed on the front burner of our lives. I write this essay as if the verse was true; you can decide, by reading further in the book, how you and the utterly enchanting concept will connect.

I divide this essay into three topics: wisdom and its allure, God's use of wisdom, and wisdom and our future.

WISDOM AND ITS ALLURE

Proverbs 16:16 stands precisely in the center of the Book of Proverbs; half of the verses precede and half follow it. This verse relates neither to those that precede or follow it. It is almost as if the author or final compiler of the collection wanted to make a point — 'lest you miss it,' he is saying, 'I will put the smack in the middle of the book.' Like a dog that stretches out in the center of the room, taking all eyes in and delighting in the attention, so wisdom's declaration is in the middle of the Book of Proverbs.

But it is also one of the first and last words of the book. Proverbs is:

"For learning about wisdom and instruction," 1:2;
"for gaining instruction in wise dealing," 1:3.
Thus:
"Let the wise hear and gain in learning," 1:5.

But it also appears as one of the traits of the good wife at the end of the book:

"She opens her mouth with wisdom," 31:26.

If, in the Muslim tradition, a newborn child is brought into the word with the *Shahadah* (profession of the Oneness of God) and a dying person is supposed to hear, as his or her last words, the words of the *Shahadah*, the wisdom tradition of Israel goes one step further—it gives us wisdom at the beginning, *middle* and end of the book.[1]

The value of wisdom is celebrated repeatedly in Proverbs. Hear the following:

> "Happy are those who find wisdom
>> and those who get understanding,
> for her income is better than silver,
>> and her revenue better than gold.
> She is more precious than jewels,
>> and nothing you desire can compare with her.
> Long life is in her right hand;
>> in her left hand are riches and honor.
> Her ways are ways of pleasantness,
>> and all her paths are peace.
> She is a tree of life to those who lay hold of her;
>> those who hold her fast are called happy,"
>
> 3:13-18.

---

1   The point I am making is literary, not theological or polemical. From a theological perspective, any good Muslim recites the Shahadah daily. It isn't just the music to bring a person in and out of the world. The Shahadah is one of the five pillars of Islam. Indeed, in my judgment, the regularity of prayer and the goal of pilgrimage and the annual feast of Ramadan give Islam such a level of practical power and appeal that one can only admire its ability in capturing the minds and hearts of people as well as providing a complete cultural understanding to its adherents.

This macarism (note that it begins and ends with "happy") is meant to stimulate the quest for wisdom. Wisdom should be treasured, and it should be sought. From the preceding chapter:

"My child, if you accept my words,
    and treasure up my commandments within you,
making your ear attentive to wisdom
    and inclining your heart to understanding;
if you seek it like silver,
    and search for it as for hidden treasures—
then you will understand the fear of the Lord
    and find the knowledge of God.
For the Lord gives wisdom…," 2:1-5.

We are not only to store it up, but we are never to forget it:

"Let your heart hold fast my words;
    keep my commandments, and you will live.
Get wisdom; get insight;
    do not forget nor turn away from the words of
    my mouth.
Do not forsake her, and she will keep you;
    love her, and she will guard you," 4:4-6.

This is enough to show that, according to the Book of Proverbs, the desire, quest and guarding of wisdom is the most important task in life. Sometimes the words are expressed as an exhortation to young people, but the entire tenor of Proverbs is that wisdom is a lifelong pursuit. Wisdom, then, is simply the most important thing in the world.

How earnestly are we to pursue its lessons? The Babylonian

Talmud gives us this unforgettable line, quoted in some of the commentaries.

"A person who repeats the lesson 100 times is not to be compared with the person who repeats it 101 times."[2]

Each repetition, each attempt to master the lessons of wisdom is qualitatively different from the last, for each new attempt at mastery fixes it more deeply into the marrow of our being.

GOD LOOKS TO WISDOM TOO

According to Proverbs, when God was creating the world, wisdom was ever by God's side, helping out in the process. Proverbs 8 is the classic text on this one. Actually, the presentation of wisdom in 8:22-31 is so striking that most scholars speak of wisdom as almost a semi-divine entity.[3] Wisdom in Proverbs is both practical advice and world-shaping principle. Here it is the latter. The Pythagoreans, an ancient Greek group, said that at the heart of the universe were the rhythms of music; the author of Proverbs would say that the foundational principle of the universe is wisdom.

In Proverbs 8, wisdom speaks as if personified. She cries in the street, urging the simple to "learn prudence" and "acquire intelligence," 8:5. Wisdom is full of "good advice and sound

2　Hagigah 9b.
3　The technical term for this, in the history of Biblical Studies, is called the *hypostatization* of wisdom. Don't fear. The word is just a transliteration of the underlying Greek word, which is best translated as "substance" or "independent existent entity."

wisdom." She has "insight" and "strength," 8:14. Kings rule by wisdom, and rulers decree what is just. Then, after touting the earthly virtues of wisdom, the tone of Proverbs 8 changes. Wisdom, actually, was set up at the beginning or as the beginning of God's work. Before there were heavens or springs of water, before the mountains had been shaped:

> "then I was beside him, like a master worker
>> and I was daily his delight
> rejoicing before him always," 8:30.

Wisdom is so important for humans because it became the guiding principle of God's work in creation. The charming reference to the "master worker"[4] led generations of Christian interpreters to construe the "wisdom" her as a prototype of Christ, who was in the beginning with God and through whom all things were made.[5]

WISDOM AND OUR FUTURE

If there is one thing that occupies the minds of many even more than the present, it is the future. We make our plans and have our worries. But wisdom wants to be right there in the center of that future. In stirring language we are exhorted:

> "My child, eat honey, for it is good,
>> and the drippings of the honeycomb are sweet to
>> your taste.
> Know that wisdom is such to your soul;

---

4   The translation is disputed, though most commentators on Proverbs render it something like this.

5   John 1:1-14 is the basis of this Christian interpretation.

if you find it, you will find a future,
and your hope will not be cut off," 24:13-14.

The thought is almost identical to the previous chapter:

"Do not let your heart envy sinners,
    but always continue in the fear of the Lord.
Surely there is a future,
    and your hope will not be cut off," 23:18.

Convinced yet of wisdom's value? Let's try another approach to wisdom, this time exploring *wisdom's power.*

Day Three

PROVERBS 21:22 AND THE IRONY OF WISDOM'S POWER

"One wise person went up against a city of warriors,
and brought down the stronghold in which they
trusted," 21:22.

EVEN THOUGH THE ENGLISH TRANSLATION of the
New Revised Standard Version is crisp and clear, the verse
just quoted is 19 words in English and only 7 in Hebrew. How
can that be? Because Hebrew is a language of compressed
suggestiveness, where one verb might take as many as 5 words in
English to translate it. Sometimes an object or a preposition is not
included in Hebrew; the text assumes that the reader will supply
the meaning. This can lead to some ambiguity in translation; it
also allows the reader to "cooperate," as it were, with the text so
that you have the conscious feeling that you are building meaning
with the text as you read it in Hebrew.

A literal reading of the Hebrew of 21:22 is as follows:

"City of warriors, a wise man went up, and he brought down the stronghold of trust." By placing the "city of warriors" at the beginning of the verse, the author wants us to be thinking, in the first instance, not of a *person* but of a daunting *spectacle*. In the first colon, the wise person "goes up" (the literal meaning of the term is a movement upwards, such as climbing a mountain or mounting the steps of the Temple in Jerusalem). The preposition "against" is missing, but we easily fill in the word. In fact, however, until we get to the second colon, we aren't really sure if the wise man is just going up *to* the city of warriors or is going *against* such a city.

Thus, the crucial word in the entire verse is the fifth word, "and he brought down." The verb is a very simple one, but its meaning is unassailably clear—the wise man conquered the fortified city through his wisdom. The wise one trusted in the sources of his own strength—wisdom—and he brought down the sources of the city's trust—its mighty soldiers.

By examining the verbs of 21:22 we see that it is a proverb of movement, up and down. The wise goes up; the result of the going up is the bringing down. A wave-like movement is envisioned. This, in fact, is similar to the flow of Ps. 107:26, where sailors, who went down to the sea in ships:

> "mounted up to heavens, (and then)
>   they went down to the depths.."

We are mesmerized by the movements of the wise person and the collapse of the walls of the city. There he goes up against the city. There go the walls, event though the walls are defended by great warriors. The significant point is that the power of wisdom trumps physical strength. The proverb is stating quite unequivocally that wisdom is more powerful than the strongest fighting force known in antiquity—the city of warriors.

REFLECTING ON POWERFUL FORCES

If you were asked to make a list of the most powerful things in the world, you probably wouldn't put "wisdom" at the top of the list. Love would be a popular selection; the US military another; the moral strength of a people would be a third; fear might be a fourth. While not explicitly saying that wisdom is the most powerful force in the world, the author leaves us to infer from the text that it is.

This idea is expressed elsewhere in Scripture, though the word "wisdom" isn't used in the description. The Psalmist says (18:29):

> "By you (God) I can crush a troop,
> and by my God I can leap over a wall,"

The story of the young and relatively defenseless shepherd boy David against the swaggering power of the powerful Philistine warrior Goliath also illustrates the point (I Sam 17). David's "wisdom" consisted in laying aside the armor of Saul in favor of the five smooth stones as he entered into battle with the warrior. He went up not just against the "city of warriors" but the "mountain man warrior" and brought him down with one well-placed stone. Such stories no doubt lie behind the proverb so eloquently stated in 21:22.

A SKEPTICAL WORD

Proverbs 21:22 is the only proverb actually ruminated on by

a later biblical book, Ecclesiastes. As you may know, Ecclesiastes is the great skeptic or, more accurately stated, the one who has experienced all of life's pleasures and pains, and simply hesitates to embrace many of the clear principles of Proverbs without equivocation. Listen to what The Preacher does to 21:22:

> "I have also seen this example of wisdom under the sun, and it seemed great to me. There was a little city with few people in it. A great king came against it and besieged it, building great siegeworks against it. Now there was found in it a poor wise man, and he by his wisdom delivered the city. Yet no one remembered that poor man. So I said, 'Wisdom is better than might; yet the poor man's wisdom is despised, and his words are not heeded,'" Ecclesiastes 9:13-16.

Ecclesiastes accepts the premise of Proverbs, but then turns it on its head. Let us assume, he says, that a man delivered a city by his wisdom. Rather than bringing down a city by wisdom, the man delivered it by wisdom. Pretty equivalent. But the result was that no one honored the wise man after the city was delivered. They just forget him. What, then, is the value of wisdom if no one will recognize you for it after you show it? This correlates well with Ecclesiastes' skeptical approach to wealth. You can have all the wealth in the world (even be as rich as Solomon), but you don't know whether the person to whom you bequeath it will be a fool or not. The person may squander it or use it unwisely; all the work put into amassing it will be lost.

Ecclesiastes is not questioning the premise of Proverbs—

that wisdom is the most powerful force in the world, but is questioning the value of wisdom. What is so valuable about wisdom if people follow your advice and then forget you are the one who provided it? Perhaps another person wants to take credit for the advice; perhaps there are people all around who are just waiting to take the words you formulate and use them for their benefit and advancement.

CONCLUSION—A PERSONAL COMMENT

When I decided to write this book, I also made the decision to make its premise the central premise of my life—that wisdom is the mastery of life's circumstances and that gaining wisdom is the most valuable activity in the world. I committed myself to the ideas laid out in the rest of this book—that I should ponder rather than speak, that I should be slow to anger, patient in taking abuse, careful in dealing with the fool, but vigorous in confronting the mocker or scoffer. I have tried for a long time to organize my life in such a way that much time can be spent on the cultivation and application of wisdom. When I committed myself to that with all my heart, I discovered a sense of personal power, clarity and satisfaction that I never before have experienced. Insights come to me, words are there, problems that have bedeviled others with whom I work are not such problems anymore. In short, I have decided to consider that wisdom *is* the most powerful thing in the world, have prayed for its gift, have tried to live with it in my heart and on my mind, and have benefited from it. The only other thing to add, however, is the word from Ecclesiastes. I may have to get used to the notion that wisdom can come forth from my lips and then be fully or largely ignored. That, then, is the question of faith for me; do I seek wisdom for its intrinsic value and inherent worth, or do I only seek it because of the benefits it might provide? In that question is the debate between Proverbs and Ecclesiastes, but one thing they don't disagree on is that wisdom is the most powerful force in the world.

We can only test the truth of Proverbs 21:22 if we decided to commit ourselves to the life of wisdom. Seek wisdom today rather than gold, rather than approbation, rather than the many things that might otherwise take your time. If my experience is any guide, your life will never be the same.

Day Four

PROVERBS 24:3-4 AND
A DREAM OF WISDOM

"By wisdom a house is built,
   and by understanding it is established;
by knowledge the rooms are filled,
   with all precious and pleasant riches," 24:3-4.

O N FIRST GLANCE these verses seem rather pedestrian.
They pick up on the theme of wisdom's building a home
or palace in 9:1; they seem to refer back to God's creative act of
"building" the universe in 3:19-20. Those latter verses read:

"The Lord by wisdom founded the earth;
   by understanding he established the heavens;
by his knowledge the deeps broke open,
   and the clouds drop down the dew."

Doesn't Proverbs 24:3-4 echo 3:19-20? Just as God builds

the universe by wisdom, and brings forth the deeps by knowledge, so we build our own "universe" (in this case our "house") by wisdom and fill its rooms with knowledge. This appears to be the end of the story. We imitate God in our quest for wisdom and knowledge.

All this might be true literarily and even theologically, but the passage didn't really come home to me personally until I realized that it cast light on a long-perplexing dream I had. In the remainder of this essay I would like to share that dream and then reflect on dreams and truth with a comment on John Bunyan's classic *Pilgrim's Progress* (1678).

MY DREAM

My dream may have been triggered by a house-hunting expedition in the summer of 1990. I had just been offered a teaching job at a small Kansas college, and my wife and I were in Kansas, from Oregon, to meet the faculty of the college and check out housing possibilities. So small was the town that when we decided to spend the day house-hunting, we were told by our realtor that there were really only two homes for sale in town that would fit our (rather minimal) needs. One was a Victorian home, built circa 1900, selling for the whopping price of $58,000. We eventually chose the other (newer) home, in an *upscale* neighborhood, for $60,000. Though happy with the newer home, I could never quite get the Victorian home out of my mind.

Sometime after that I had a dream. I dreamed I was in the front yard of a large Victorian home. It was a massive structure, multi-colored, with large wrap-around porch, flanked by bay windows and a cantilevered second floor, covered with a front-facing gable over the south part of the house. Above the gable was a spindly-shaped finial, pointing heavenward. On the north side of the house, over the porch, was a turret, rising to the height of about thirty feet. I stood admiring the house, taking in its majesty and splendor.

Then I climbed the seven steps to the porch and was surprised to see my name on the plate below the mailbox. I tried the door and it opened. I entered cautiously into the hall and then glanced into the parlor to the left. The parlor opened to a large living room on the south side of the house. I was surprised by what I saw. Instead of two rooms neatly appointed with period furniture or with my own possessions, I saw bundles of papers, huge file cabinets, piles of clothes, and furniture strewn rather irregularly through the rooms. In fact, as I looked more closely, I saw that almost every available inch of these two rooms was full of unorganized possessions. I recognized most of the things as my own, but many items were strange to me.

Then, deciding to forsake those rooms, I headed upstairs. Five bedrooms, ranging from a master suite of impressive proportions to a servant's bedroom in the rear, filled that floor. But it was completely empty. Not a bureau, desk, bed, rug, piece of furniture or clothing graced this floor. I descended a back staircase to the kitchen, and realized that the rest of the house, downstairs included, was likewise barren. Everything I owned, it seemed, was piled up in the parlor and the living room. Nothing was organized.

For years I lived with that dream, mostly ignoring it but sometimes trying to understand it in the context of human memory and information storage. When I came across Proverbs 24:3-4, however, the dream began to take on a new resonance. I saw the dream as a kind of longing, a longing for wisdom and the knowledge that would fill my "house" of wisdom. I saw my dream as a persistent invitation in my life, where I was approaching wisdom, and wisdom was indeed my own house, but where the constituent elements that made the house "work," such as beds and furniture, were completely disorganized. That is, I saw myself as a yearner for wisdom but a yearner who really was hindered in that quest because his knowledge was disorganized. I realized that what I needed to do in my life at that time, and perhaps for most of my adult life, was to take the time patiently to sort through the knowledge and deck out the rooms of the beautiful Victorian mansion with the furniture of my life—my knowledge. Yet, instead of outfitting it properly, I had been throwing valuable things aside. I might have had the longing for wisdom, and the valuable possessions that would one day materialize into knowledge, but for many years I was stacking up those valuable things in an unusable pattern.

The passage from Proverbs 24:3-4, then, became a most wonderful assurance, as well as goad, to me. I began to read it as a promise, a statement from the heart of the Scriptures, that wisdom, married with knowledge, makes a most impressive home, a most rich and full residence. It left me feeling joyful and hopeful. It has rekindled the search for knowledge and its intelligent expression in wise saying and writing.

A WORD ON PILGRIM'S PROGRESS

I am not the only one for whom a dream has provided potent personal and religious insight. John Bunyan's classic 1678 religious allegory, *Pilgrim's Progress*, is described, on the title page, as "delivered under the similitude of a dream." Note the setting of the entire work, from the first lines of this simply-written allegory:

"As I walked through the wilderness of this world,
I lighted on a certain place, where was a den; and I
laid me down in that place to sleep: and as I slept I
dreamed a dream. I dreamed..."[1]

Get the impression that "dream" is an important idea for
Bunyan? Occasionally throughout the book, Bunyan reminds
his readers that he is speaking as if in a dream; e.g., as he sees
Christian flee the City of Destruction on his way to the Heavenly
City.[2] Finally, in the last paragraph, when Vain-hope was unable
to produce his certificate for entrance into heaven and was thrown
down to hell, the story concludes, "Then I awoke, and behold it
was a dream."[3]

Bunyan, aware that using the vehicle of a dream to teach
spiritual truth was nearly anathema to his fellow Puritans, attached
a several-page "Apology" for his book at the beginning. In those
pages he defended the literary form of dream to convey truth,
arguing, among other things, that dreams were used in Scripture
to communicate spiritual insight. In addition, the Bible:

"is everywhere so full of all these things,
　　(Dark features, allegories), yet there springs
From that same book that luster and those rays
　　Of light that turns our darkest nights to days."[4]

---

1   I used the Penguin Classics edition, edited by Roger Sharrock. The
quotation is on p. 11.
2   An example is on p. 56, where Christian is passing through a frightening
valley—"I saw then in my dream..."
3   *Ibid.*, p. 142.
4   *Ibid.*, p. 6.

Dreams often teach us the truth about ourselves. Dreams can teach us about wisdom. Build your house on wisdom, fill your rooms with rich and pleasant knowledge, take time to sort out all the knowledge and perhaps you, too, will have dreams fulfilled.

The Heart of Wisdom

Day Five

ABOVE ALL, GUARD THE HEART

"Keep your heart with all vigilance, for from it flow
the springs of life," 4:23.

W E ARE A LITTLE SURPRISED that such a clear and
powerful thought appears in the middle of a long and
relatively uneventful admonition from parent to child. The first 22
verses of the fourth chapter are an earnest, but rather predictable,
collection of exhortations to listen to parental advice, to prize
wisdom and to avoid the path of the wicked. Then, just as we
were expecting the chapter to end in more of a whimper than a
bang, we are confronted with these words.

Their power comes across in English, but it is even more
pronounced in the Hebrew. We have only eight Hebrew words in
the sentence but already the first two words cut us short. Literally
they are translated "Above all watchings" or "More than anything
you watch." The Greek version of the Bible (the Septuagint)
didn't quite know what to do with this phrase, and so it rendered

it "*In* all your watchings." But the thought in Hebrew is clear even if the first word is a bit strange — the author is pointing to the *highest priority* of life. The author is saying, 'above every other thing that you tend to, cultivate the heart...' The piece of advice is like saying to the watchman of the city, 'Pay attention to the whole, but especially make sure you keep *that* house or *that* gate in your view.'

The second colon of the verse gives the reason for this arresting admonition. Literally it says, "for from it are the goings out of life." No one uses the word "goings out" to express *anything*, so we have to render it another way. It normally is translated "issues" or "springs" of life, but the form of the word, a participle, emphasizes a continuous action. Just as blood flows from the heart, so the "goings out" constantly flow from that same heart. The blood is only a physical manifestation of other things that are constantly flowing from the heart. The heart, as will be shown below, is the "command center" of life, according to the Bible. Thus, in few words, Proverbs 4:23 exhorts us to care for our heart, because it sends out the very signals of life for us. In expressing this thought, we seem to hear an adumbration of Jesus' words,

> "For out of the abundance of the heart the mouth
> speaks." Matt. 13:34.

We aren't really told what the scope of these issues or springs is, but a preliminary hint follows in 4:24-27. We are to put crooked speech away from us, and we are to keep to the straight path as we turn from evil. These two warnings will be extremely important in later essays as we look more closely at the life of the wise person, but for the remainder of this one, we will zoom in on the concept of the heart.

THE HEART IN THE OLD TESTAMENT

Since we are told to keep or tend our heart, it is probably best to explore the contours of the concept of the heart in the Hebrew Bible. As Van Leeuwen suggests, the Bible doesn't make a dichotomy between the mind and the heart.[1] The same word, *leb*, stands behind the two English words. *Leb* occurs more than 700 times in the Bible, and so any attempt at full exposition of its scope is out of the question. Though it can refer to the physical organ in the chest, of greater interest is the metaphorical use for "the internal wellspring of the acting self."[2] That is, the heart is conceived of as the motivational or the control center of life. When some action occurs in political or civic life, those who really want to understand the action ask the question, 'Who is really behind this action, and for what reason?' So it is with the heart. Whenever we manifest an attitude or perform an action, the heart stands behind it. Thus, the heart becomes the subject of so many Biblical references.

In the pessimistic (some might call it realistic) assessment of Jeremiah, "The heart is devious above all else, and beyond cure—who can understand it?" Jer. 17:9-10. Though Proverbs is mum on the extreme deviousness of the heart, it agrees with Jeremiah on the next point: only God can know it thoroughly. "I the Lord test the mind and search the heart," Jer. 17:10; cf. Prov. 21:2; 15:11. While humans look on the outward appearance in making judgments, the Lord looks on the heart, I Sam. 16:7. Though the human heart may be in rebellion against God, the

1 *Proverbs* (The New Interpreter's Bible), p. 60.
2 *Ibid.*

75

Psalmist can pray with confidence, "Search me, O God, and know my heart," Ps. 139:23. The searched heart is a prelude to the obedient heart. And, in fact, the Scriptures assure that God's plan is to give the people of God a new heart or, in Jeremiah's language, a heart on which God has written the new law:

> "I will put my law within them, and I will write it on
> their hearts; and I will be their God, and they shall
> be my people," Jer. 31:33.

Thus, when Proverbs exhorts the hearers to tend or keep the heart as the highest task, it does so against the background of a rich discussion of this control center, this foundation of human life. Van Leeuwen compares the first colon of Proverbs 4:23 with Socrates' admonition to "know thyself," and says that Proverbs goes beyond Socrates in scope and depth.[3] We know, then, that the stakes regarding the watching of the heart are immense.

HOW TO WATCH THE HEART

What, then, does Proverbs mean when it says, "Above every watching, tend the heart"? Three verbs that help clarify this thought are *guide, guard* and *govern*. If we learn to do all three, we are being faithful to the solemn charge of this verse.

Before looking briefly at each of these words, it is good to stop and consider what we are being asked to do. Normally, with matters of this import, Proverbs puts the onus for control and results in God's hands. "The king's heart is a stream of water in the hand of the Lord; he turns it wherever he will," 21:1. But here, *we* are to tend the heart. So, we tend, but God

---

3   *Ibid*, p. 61.

turns. How do we tend it? First, by *guiding* our heart. We guide it by committing ourselves to the way of wisdom. Proverbs is clear that the choice between the paths of wisdom and folly is ours; both Lady Wisdom and Lady Folly call to us, in identical language, telling us to "turn in here," Prov. 9:4, 16. So, we guide our heart by finding out all we can about the path of wisdom and committing ourselves unequivocally to its way. It is as simple and as difficult as that.

But we also need to *guard* the heart. We do so by eliminating habits that debilitate us and by protecting the heart from outside influences that will enervate. We can't guard the heart properly if we give access to it to every person that wants it. Our hearts are tender and vulnerable organs; they need to let in only those who can build it, buttress it, enlarge its scope. In addition, we must take care to guard the heart by ridding our lives of those numerous distractions and air-leaks that make us unable to function with our creativity and intellect in its fullest form.

Finally, we need to *govern* the heart. We do so by making sure not only that we have sought out the path of wisdom, but that we are putting practices into our lives that maximize our life on that path. To that end, it requires the management of what we say, how we say it, when we say it, with whom we associate, and to what we give our attention. Caring for the heart comes down to living faithfully each day, aware of the fact that each new day brings challenges to our creativity and distractions from the way of wisdom.

CONCLUSION

There is no task quite so urgent or important as tending to the heart. Its "outflow" is the way that we meet the world. To the extent that that outflow reflects a heart that is divided and confused, to that extent we sound an uncertain trumpet in the world. So, take care today to tend to the heart, to cultivate it as you would a most precious garden. The attention you pay to this task will result in gifts that the world has not yet seen from you.

Day Six

PROVERBS 14:10, 13 AND THE HEART'S BITTERNESS

"The heart knows its own bitterness, and no stranger
shares its joy," 14:10.

"Even in laughter the heart is sad, and the end of joy
is grief," 14:13.

THE PREVIOUS CHAPTER spoke of the value of the heart.
Guard it, above all things. The words of 4:23 stake out an
optimistic ground for the Book of Proverbs. And, indeed, the
popular scholarly opinion on Proverbs is that it is an optimistic
book, with brimming confidence not only in the rule of God in
the world but in the blessed life for the righteous and wise person.
And that opinion is supported by several texts.

"Long life is in her (i.e., wisdom's) right hand;
in her left hand are riches and honor," 3:16.

"The reward for humility and fear of the Lord,
   is riches and honor and life," 22:4.

These verses could be multiplied manifold. But Prov. 14:10, 13, the verses for today, take a different perspective on the human heart. These verses teach, in fact, that we are solitary creatures and that the basic condition of life, from which we emerge and to which we return after a fleeting moment of joy, is grief or sadness. We are alone, and often bereft, in our own interpretive dilemmas as we review the private "home movies" of our lives. This essay reflects on the knowability of the human heart and why it might be true that the heart's bitterness is known only to itself.

BEGINNING WITH A BIBLICAL
STORY OF BITTERNESS

Naomi married Elimilech, a man of Bethlehem, and had two sons with him. The sons grew up and married, and then they all left Bethlehem for lands in the East. All three of the men then died. Bereft of all her immediate family members, she left that region with her daughter-in-law Ruth and returned to Bethlehem. Having heard the news of her loss, the town was "stirred," Ruth 1:19. The text follows:

   "'Is this Naomi?' She said to them, 'Call me no
      longer Naomi,
   call me Mara (translating the Hebrew word meaning
      "bitter") for the Almighty has dealt bitterly with
      me," Ruth 1:19-20.

Her name, like so many Biblical names, mirrored her condition in life. So dominating was her pain that she wanted her name, bitter, to reflect it. Permanently.

THE INSCRUTABILITY OF OUR OWN HEARTS

We meet a person. We may meet him or her at work, in a common task, in almost any situation. There sits the person. Hair is usually coiffed. Clothes are clean. Most people in this situation try to present an air of calmness and assurance, a feeling of control and comfort. The person lives in the present, and has longings for the future, but what actually confronts you is a person who is the sum of his or her *past*. The scars here and there, the tattoos visible peeking out from the shirts, are just external signs of an internal scarring or marking work that has been taking place for years.

The person as she or he meets you is a bundle of emotions, experiences, skills, memories and longings. Though you might want them to do a task for you, if you are hiring them, or to engage with you, if you are trying to connect personally with them, they are, as they sit there, fundamentally the product of their scarred past. Even if you do a "30 minute tour" of their lives, and skillfully ask questions about their favorite teacher, past pets, the movie most indelibly fixed in their minds, their biggest obstacle or failure, you will understand only the thinnest veneer covering their lives. And that veneer of those events is itself covered through the cloudy interpretive film of the present. In fact, when we present ourselves to others, we do so as solitary creatures, alone in a complex web of unresolved losses and griefs, trying vainly to put them to rest or, at least, to still their voices for the moment so that we can get on with our lives and answer questions posed to us.

The claim of Proverbs 14:10 is that these experiences from our past make our heart basically inaccessible to other people. "The heart knows its own bitterness." The heart alone. How can that be? If I, the interviewer, "played ball" at "State U," and the interviewee also "played ball" at "State U" or maybe at "elite private college," why doesn't the similarity of experience provide a sort of "match" that not only links us in friendship but joins the heart? Because of the way that experiences are fixed on the mind and heart. Let me illustrate.

Let us assume that a child experiences a moment either of rejection or of joy. It might be the joy of sitting by the fire at the grandparents cabin in the cold of an autumn night, but the feeling of coziness is so strong and the resonance of love so rich, that the child feels extremely cherished, and is completely at peace with the world. The child later relates that experience, but even as there is joy in telling it, there is a bit of pain because it has disappeared forever. He or she experiences a sort of nostalgia, a word invented about 400 years ago in English, and taken directly from the Greek, to express the "pain" (*algia*) and "going home" (*nostos*) that is familiar to people. And then, in the telling of the story, there are other features that make this experience, though common to many, unique to the individual. The unique features of the experience then cause it to sink, as it were, into diffuse caverns of our memory. Our memory becomes filled with not only the memories of the event, but of the glasses as they rest on grandma's nose, the clothes grandpa used to wear, the layout of the room, the colors of the rugs, the decorations that remind us of holiday special times. Each common experience of true joy or grief from the past is encased in a plenitude of other features that give the experience a unique cast and tint. Perhaps this was the last time we saw grandpa alive. Maybe they sold the cabin shortly thereafter. Perhaps some event happened in the child's life that made this event especially memorable.

In addition, the events that happen in the past reach different people at diverse levels because of the varied sensitivities to the meanings of the events that people have. When talking with my brothers at a family reunion, we often reminisce about childhood days in Connecticut when our father worked in NYC and we were successful students and athletes in the public schools. But all of us have slightly skewed memories of dad, who died in the 1980s. One of the brothers still feels the sting and hurt of dad's critical comments; another is more forgiving of dad's occasional harshness because dad helped him learn how to become a better trumpet player. Though each of us experienced the same parents in the same house for many years, we have profoundly different memories of how the parents shaped us, and our reaction to these.

Then, as we grow older, the distances between people grow even greater. It is as if we all begin, in the womb, at a very similar place in life, just enjoying the mother's nourishment as it pulsates to us. But then it is as if we all emerge from the womb and begin to take different roads, roads that ramify from each other and keep spreading into an unlimited space, like the broad branching limbs of a great oak or sycamore. We may make connections with people along the way, but fundamentally those connections are only temporarily "crossings" of the branches, and the branch that is myself stays rather untouched from all the other branches in the world.

And what of the experience of loss? On one occasion I lost a ring, which belonged to my grandfather, which he received on his 16th birthday, in 1917. To no one else would the ring mean something. But it meant something to me, and my loss of it not only evoked all kinds of memories of my grandfather, but the deepest sort of pain at my carelessness and negligence for the loss of this object. Others have lost rings, and many have lost things of much greater significance than that. But my loss highlighted the fact that the grief I felt in response could not only not be assuaged by anyone else, but couldn't really be understood by another.

Because only our heart can truly know our own bitterness and grief, it is as if, in many ways, the rest of the world becomes "strangers" to us (the word in the second colon of 14:10). All are strangers, and they, who couldn't share our grief, are also unable really to partake of our joy. We are solitary in our triumphs, even as the accolades fly and the confetti falls on us. In fact, as Proverbs 14:13 suggests, grief is the identity-shaping experience of our lives, and we emerge into the spotlight of joy only long enough to pick up the trophy, before we return to our depths.

CONCLUSION

These verses present Proverbs' strongest case for the inscrutability or unknowability of the human heart. We think we know someone else, but even if we have been united to that person for years there is a dimension of sad distance which causes a chasm between us. And, who is to say, in the last analysis, whether we really know *our own hearts?* We have constant tapes playing in our mind, both audio and video, of our past, but these tapes change as we hear them again. An event from one era takes on new meaning when we revisit it later in life. Our past is as plastic as our future, and the stronger the hermeneutical grid we place over our past, the more it becomes almost as uncertain as our future. We emerge, then, from ignorance and experiences that communicate ambiguous meanings. We merge with others, and share their ambiguous experiences and ignorance. We look forward to a future where clarity is only longed-for and rarely realized. Thus, when the final chapter is written, and the roll is called up yonder, we may know ourselves so little that we may barely be able to respond to our own names. And Proverbs tells us that what we will know of ourselves, the bitterness and the joy, will basically be locked away in our own hearts, hidden in the deep caves of our own memories. God, indeed, may know the heart and try the heart, as other verses in Proverbs teach, but we only share that heart and life with God. When we think about this last point for a moment, perhaps we can understand the 'good news' of one of the verses in between our two quoted verses from Proverbs.

"The house of the wicked is destroyed,
    but the tent of the upright flourishes," 14:11.

Perhaps even though our hearts are inscrutable and the grief returns, we will flourish. That is the powerful and hopeful realism of the Book of Proverbs.

Day Seven

PROVERBS 20:5 AND THE KNOWABILITY
OF THE HUMAN HEART

"The purposes in the human mind are like deep water,
but the intelligent will draw them out," 20:5.

THIS ESSAY DEALS WITH another side of the issue
broached in the previous chapter. There I argued, from
14:10,13, that each individual is immured in his or her own
prison of pain and grief, and that no matter how much we try to
connect with one another, the human heart remains inaccessible
to us. Yet that isn't the end of the story—by a long fashion.
Proverbs also believes that there may be special avenues to reach
that apparently inaccessible heart. In this case the intelligent or
discerning or wise person will draw a person out.[1] In this essay I

---

1   Half of the 30 or so Bibilcal appearances of the Hebrew word *tebunah*,
translated here as "intelligent," appear in Proverbs. *Tebunah* is one of the
cluster of words associated with wisdom or insight. Proverbs 2:2 is an example:
"making your ear attentive to wisdom and inclining your heart to understanding
(*tebunah*)."

explore the contours of the "deep water" of 20:5 and the process of "drawing" another person "out" of that water.

UNDERSTANDING THE "FLOW" OF THE VERSE

The crucial words to understand in the verse are "deep waters" and "draw them out." Obviously the metaphor is taken from the common agricultural experience of drawing water from a well, but something needs to be said about the Hebrew word translated "deep" (*amukim*). What does it mean that human purposes are deep? On the one hand one can argue that it simply means profound or unfathomable. When we say, "She is a deep person," we mean that it is difficult to figure her out or that she is always bringing the mind to bear on an issue in an interesting way.

But here the word *amukim* means something more than that—and that "more" is crucial for our understanding. In short *amukim* carries with it the notion of being sinister, dangerous and cunning. Jeremiah talked about the heart of humans being desperately corrupt (17:9), and the linguistic reach of *amukim* here isn't too far removed from that. The word appears only 16 times in the Bible. Seven of these appearances, interestingly enough, are in Leviticus 13, to describe a leprosy that is deeper than the skin. But the other appearances connect *amukim* with death, darkness and insidious human plans. Job 11:8 speaks of the depths of the grave; Job 12:22 of the depths of darkness that must be revealed. It is used with the phrase "deep pit" in Proverbs to describe the ways of the harlot (22:14; 23:17). Psalm 64:6 uses it in the sense of evil plans. Here is Ps. 64:6 in context:

"They (the wicked) hold fast to their evil purpose;

they talk of laying snares secretly,
thinking, 'Who can see us?'
Who can search out our crimes?
We have thought out a cunningly conceived plot."
For the human heart and mind are deep *(amok)*."
64:5-6.

Thus, we are justified in seeing *amukim* in 20:5 to describe the rather sinister depths of the human heart. Proverbs 18:4 also uses the phrase "deep waters" to contrast with the ways of wisdom:

"The words of the mouth are deep waters;
the fountain of wisdom is a gushing stream."[2]

Thus, our verse *begins* where we left off in our consideration of 14:10, 13. The human heart is inaccessible, cunning, filled with grief, remote. But then the tone changes. A person of understanding or wisdom can "draw out" such a heart. The verb translated "draw out" is very rare in the Bible, appearing only about five times. The two most visual uses of the word are in Exodus 2:16, 19, where the Midianites or Egyptians are said to draw water out of a well. Thus, 20:5 stresses that an understanding person can draw out the cunning, confusingly profound and seemingly unsearchable plans and intentions of the human heart. How does this happen? Wouldn't the person who is able to draw out the deep things of the human heart be the most valuable person in the world?

2   There is debate among scholars whether the two cola of 18:4 are meant to be understood as adversatives or complements. Either translation is grammatically possible. Most leading translations assume an adversative, as I do here. Waltke discusses the issue in *The Book of Proverbs, 15-31*, pp. 71-72.

THE ART OF THE INTERVIEW

Proverbs doesn't directly tell us *how* the intelligent person draws out the heart of another. But I think we can derive some clues from reflection on life experience as well as studying the way leading interviewers try to derive information from others. After all, shouldn't they be skilled at drawing out information from the profound and sometimes cunning depths of the heart?

An online article gets us started.[3] Entitled "The Art of the Interview, ESPN-Style," it mentions that ESPN, the sports network, has hired the accomplished journalism professor John Sawatsky to help its interviewers learn how to ask better questions of interviewees. ESPN executives felt that they had lost lots of stories because their reporters couldn't quite get to the heart of an issue with a subject. Hence, the hiring of Sawatsky. His tips on how to conduct an interview that draws people out are worth quoting.

> "Sawatsky's rules are simple, but he says they get broken all the time: Don't ask yes-or-no questions, keep questions short and avoid charged words, which can distract people."

The bottom line for Sawatsky is for the interviewer truly to consider the *other* as the more important person in the encounter. This philosophy, he argues, will enable the interviewer to get candid responses.

---

3   https://www.npr.org/templates/story/story.php?storyId=5625218

MY OWN METHOD

Over the years, I have developed a system of sorts in drawing people out of the isolation or inscrutability of their hearts. This works for me in about 90% of cases; I readily admit I can't reach about 10% of people. It is useful whether or not I have a long relationship with another, but it is especially helpful if I have just met the other person. It is built on wisdom principles and consists of three steps: (1) Eliminate the potential hostility; (2) Show knowledge of something vital and rare shared by the other; (3) Share select important details of one's own life. If these are done well, and wisely, the heart of another generally opens up to me.

1) The principle I call "Eliminating the potential hostility" emerges from the realization that every encounter of humans begins with an element of fear. We don't always know the intentions of the other, and our natural inclination in meeting others is to make sure that we are protected. Indeed, many of us have lived "unprotected" relational lives over the years and have paid dearly for it. So, I assume that each person I meet not only is a treasure trove of information and knowledge, but is inaccessible to me at first because there are probably unspoken fears that have to be addressed. First, then, we need to remove the fear. You don't necessarily do it with a smile, though that doesn't hurt. Fear is eliminated primarily through expressions of good will that make sure the other is comfortable. It can be through an observation about the person, but often it is a comment on the situation in which you both find yourselves, or a statement that shows that you are a "safe" person. Much, much more could be said about this step.

2) Showing Knowledge. This is the step that needs most

time to cultivate. You draw out another person's heart, you bring them out of their potential evil plans or unsearchable confusion, if you demonstrate knowledge about unique things in their lives. But how can this be, since you have just met them? It can be because you have so studied the world, its geography, history, the general life patterns of most people, that you just happen to be able to find and connect with a point of knowledge the other has in his or her past which is both important to the person and which others know nothing about. The result of this method, after you practice it, is reactions by others that say, "I don't know how you know that!" or "I don't know why I am telling you this but...." A fairly trite example will make the point. I once met a person from Billings, Montana. I had only driven through Billings once in my life, and had few memories of it. But I had studied a lot, and remembered that the address of a college that I wanted to learn about was on Rimrock Road in Billings. So, I knew only one thing about the town. When the person mentioned that s/he was from Billings, I gently inquired whether it was in the neighborhood of Rimrock Road. You would have thought that I was the person's best friend—or became that. Stories began to flow of the person's past, friends they knew, memories they had, people who meant something to them from their earlier days.

This example may be infinitely multiplied. I was in Saudi Arabia in January 1993 and was sitting at a formal dinner next to a turbaned, distinguished man. Fortunately, he spoke English (this is the argument for learning as many languages as you can...). I had studied some of the history of the country before visiting it, and had learned some of the significant family names in that country's modern history. Since it is a small country in population, I only memorized about 50 names, with some reference to why each family was important. So, we began to speak. I noticed his nametag. I asked him if he was related to a man who led an unsuccessful rebellion against King Abdul Aziz back in the 1920s. Immediately, his eyes lit up, "How do you know about *that*?" He then proceeded to tell me all kinds of information about the earlier desert life of his family, the struggles, the factions before independence, etc. Doors of real understanding and sharing were opened.

3) The previous step is a knowledge-seeking step. It can only work if you are a lover of knowledge and are attentive to the way that knowledge can be used to draw people out of their distresses and their private worlds. But these steps must be complemented by a personal transparency, a willingness to share details of your own life with another, a willingness to make honesty and straightforwardness be the currency of exchange between you. You don't have to share all your intimate details; indeed, you probably shouldn't, but there are enough important things you can bring to another that can function to draw them out from their potential heart-inaccessability.

CONCLUSION

I was a bit hesitant, in constructing this chapter, to share some of my wisdom-based interview method lest it become the subject of ridicule or attack. After all, some might say, "Bill, what you have here is a wonderful scheme to manipulate people." Knowledge, to be sure, can be used for those purposes, but it also can be used to pry open hearts that would like to be opened. My philosophy is that openness of heart is the prelude for personal advances, in knowledge, wisdom, connections with others and finding your way in the world.

The final word is that Proverbs 20:5 is a tremendously

optimistic word. It believes that the right kind of person, with the right method of operation, can draw out another from his or her inaccessibility. It is worth a try.

Day 8

PROVERBS 27:19; 20:27: FACES AND WATER, SPIRITS AND LAMPS

"Just as water reflects the face,
    so one human heart reflects another," 27:19.

"The human spirit is the lamp of the Lord,
    searching every innermost part," 20:27.

THESE VERSES, CRYPTIC at first glance, present the most optimistic case in Proverbs for the view that the human heart is accessible and knowable.   The first verse appears in a discussion of friendship, and the key word "face" links 27:19 with a nearby verse, 27:17. A literal translation of 27:17 is:

"Iron sharpens iron,
    and one person sharpens the face of another."[1]

---

1   The NRSV, perhaps not believing the incredible directness of the word "face" here, translates the typical Hebrew word for face, *paney* (in the construct form) as "wits."

95

Thus, as iron "sharpens" other iron, so the human heart reflects itself to the other. The second verse appears in the context of things the king does. Kings search out everything (cf. 25:2), and so does the human spirit.[2] When we look more carefully at each verse in turn, we see the dramatic and comforting claims they make.

PROVERBS 27:19

A literal translation will get us started. "As water reflects the face to the face, so [is] the heart of a person to a person." The Hebrew verse consists of only seven words, and four of the seven are "face-face" and "person-person." A fifth is the comparative word "thus," and the sixth and seventh are terms that form the basis of the comparison—waters and heart. The author of this proverb is thinking about the meaning of a common human experience, looking at your face in the water. The water reflects the face back to the face. That is the simple meaning of the first three Hebrew words. Just like the face of a human is reflected back to the human through the medium of water, so the heart of a person (is reflected) to a person.

A clarification must here be sought. Since the face that is reflected is the *same* face that sees, and thus the reflecting act only involves one person, should we assume that the heart that is reflected means that it is only reflected to the owner of the heart and not another person? If this were the meaning, we would still have an optimistic proverb, though it would only be saying that ultimately the human heart is known to itself. Yet, that reading, though possible, is questionable for two reasons. First, as

2   Waltke translates the word *neshmah*, usually rendered as "breath" or "spirit" as "words," justifying it by the context of proverb—it is about thoughts or ideas searching out or bringing deep places to light.

mentioned above, the verse appears in the context of friendship. Thus, two people or more are in view. Second, Proverbs has the following verse, located not far from our second verse of the essay:

"All our steps are ordered by the Lord,
how then can we understand our own ways?" 20:24.

Thus, it probably is better to understand 27:19 as suggesting that hearts of people are known or seen by each other.[3] We see our reflection in the water; humans see the hearts of each other. Think further about faces and water. Sometimes if we see undisturbed water, it is limpid and the image or reflection is clear; sometimes it is occluded or blocked by turgid rushing waters; sometimes it is temporarily clouded through a gust of wind that ripples the surface. The verse holds out the possibility that hearts can be understood between people. Every time you see the clear reflection of your face in the water, take it as a promise of God that people are knowable. As the rainbow was to Noah (a promise by God of safety), so the waters are to us (a promise by God of knowability).

There is, at times, nothing so comforting as the realization that we are known. The Psalmist knows this feeling.

"O Lord, you have searched me and known me.
You know when I sit down and when I rise up;
you discern my thoughts from far away...

---

3   There is a certain degree of irony, however, in the idea that we can know the hearts of others while our own remain hidden to ourselves. But the concept isn't foreign. Often people are able to help others but not help themselves; to see others but not recognize themselves. We now see how Proverbs can bring us into its own fascinating web of complementary meanings.

Search me, O God, and know my heart;
　　test me and known my thoughts,"
　　　　　　　　　　　Psalm 139:1-2, 23.

Knowledge of God comes via the face. Paul argues:

"For it is the God who said, 'Let light shine out of
　　darkness,' who
has shown in our hearts to give the light of the
　　knowledge of the glory of God in the face of
　　Jesus Christ," II Corinthians 4:6.

Faces and knowledge. Faces reveal knowledge. Faces open the heart. One of the most significant modern theologians is Cambridge University's David Ford. The heart of his theological work can rightly be called a "theology of faces."[4] Not only does he ruminate extensively on the notion of the face as the giver of identity and the holder of memory, but he argues that the existence of faces means that the concept of "facing" must be taken seriously. He says,

"'Facing' helps to avoid the wrong sort of fixations on
the face as an 'object.' It embraces the face in activity
and passivity, purpose and temporality, loneliness
and reciprocity. It can be a joint conception—facing
something together. Or it can refer to interiority,
facing oneself, one's past, present and future. At its
most general it can refer to environments, institutions,
nations, or even civilizations 'facing' situations,
challenges or possibilities."[5]

4　I specifically refer here to his 1999 work *Self and Salvation* (Cambridge UP).
5　*Ibid.*, p. 23.

The possibilities inherent in the idea of the face, then, are numerous. In Proverbs 27:19 the concept of the face is one of tremendous optimism. We see our own face in the mirror-like surface of the water; so we know that a person's heart is accessible to us in the same way. We don't have to be a wise or intelligent person to "draw them up" (cf. Proverbs 20:5; see previous essay); the face and the heart of the person is available to us. But how does that person become accessible? That is where 20:27 comes in.

PROVERBS 20:27

The NRSV translation is given at the beginning of this essay. I will hold to it, even though Waltke, a significant modern reader of Proverbs, renders *neshmah*, translated by the NRSV as "spirit," as "words." The point is not insignificant. Waltke's translation would then read, "The words of a human being are the lamp of the Lord..." His translation yields a statement which is probably true, but if we recognize the creative, evocative, somewhat elusive language of Proverbs, we do the text a disservice by rushing from the inchoate "spirit" to the very determinative "words." Let's leave the word *neshmah*, which is almost always translated "spirit" or "breath" elsewhere (Gen. 2:7; Job 32:8; 33:4, etc.) as "spirit" here. So we have, in the first colon, "The spirit of a person is the lamp of the Lord." Actually, the Hebrew words are inverted: "The lamp of the Lord is the spirit of a person" but our translation makes more sense in English.

What might this mean? For Waltke the phrase would mean that our words are the way of access to the other person's innermost parts. They are the divine searchlight, the mode for perceiving the thoughts and intentions of the heart. I contend here that it is our "spirit" which acts as the great "heart-opener."

What do I mean by the translation I adopt? It is not simply our words that open another, but the entire way we present ourselves to the world that pries them/it open. We are aware, as is Proverbs, that body-language communicates as strongly, or stronger, than words. Proverbs says, for example:

"A scoundrel and a villain
    goes around with crooked speech,
winking the eyes, shuffling the feet,
    pointing the fingers...
There are six things that the Lord hates,
    seven that are an abomination to him:
haughty eyes, a lying tongue,
    and hands that shed innocent blood,
a heart that devises wicked plans,
    and feet that hurry to run to evil," 6:12-13, 16-18.

Thus, from the perspective of Proverbs there is much more to communication than simply one's words. It is the spirit of a person which is behind the words, the gestures, the way one notices things, observes the world, finds one's "fit" with life.

It is the spirit of a human which is the Lord's lamp. Psalms picks up on the notion of the Lord's lamp when it says,

"Your word is a lamp to my feet
    and a light to my path," 119:105.

God's word, then, functions as the lamp, the lamp which is our spirit, the spirit which then searches the innermost parts.

100

The Hebrew word translated "searches out" is used for a diligent search, such as when Joseph searched for the household gods of his brothers when they went to Egypt (Gen. 44:12).

This is a most optimistic verse about the knowability of the human heart because it not only suggests that it is the entire spirit of a person which performs the search (and not just the "words"), but that the spirit is, as it were, guided by the word of God. We aren't told much more than that. The verse isn't qualified by any words about wisdom being the key, or about understanding being necessary. It simply says that the spirit of a human searches the innermost parts.

CONCLUSION

So, what will it be? Is the human spirit, and is our own heart, beyond the realm of knowability? Or, does skillful application of our spirit open up that heart? Sometimes it appears like the heart is a prison, other times as a prism. Sometimes it seems to hide and absorb light; other times it reflects it. The paradox of knowing and being known, of hiding and being hid, is neatly resolved by the Apostle Paul, when speaking about love. Love, he says, is "patient; love is kind; love is not envious or boastful," I Corinthians 13:4. But then, in the great peroration of the chapter, he turns to the subject of knowing and being known:

> "Now I know only in part, then I will know fully,
> even as I have been fully known," 13:12.

Perhaps the dilemma of knowledge and hiddenness will only be resolved at the end, when we are fully known. In the meantime, we struggle with the rippling water, sometimes seeing only dim reflections of ourselves and others. In the meantime, sometimes the lamp that searches others seems to have a dull wattage indeed. But we live and we struggle, striving for knowledge and understanding. Though we may not know much when we leave this world, we may yet know that we are loved, and that we can know another's heart sufficiently to love them. That, friends, is enough. That, too, is the paradoxical spirit of Proverbs.

Meet the Fool

Day Nine

THINKING ABOUT THE FOOL

INTRODUCTION

THE FOOL PLAYS A SIGNIFICANT ROLE in the Book of Proverbs. As we will see in the next few essays, the fool is one who blusters, blunders, bludgeons, bloviates, blisters, blabs, blets, babbles and bursts. The fool is never called a wicked person, but s/he breaks the bonds of civility and community in attitude, action and speech. Thus, the fool is condemned in the most vehement terms in Proverbs; e.g., "Fools die for lack of sense," 10:21. The Biblical notion of the fool is stronger than our contemporary use of the word to disparage, contemn or express disdain for someone. We generally think of a fool today as somebody who lacks judgment and thus brings (avoidable) pain on himself. Proverbs has a much more supple and subtle characterization of the fool. The fool, for Proverbs, is not simply a pitiable but harmless person. The fool erodes the fabric of a community through arrogance, untimely words, and provocative action. Proverbs' description of the fool provides a wonderful template to lay over the world in which we live. Once we do so, conversations of all kinds begin to make more sense; people's public conduct becomes explicable; even the decisions of politicians and political entities are more clearly understood. The purpose of these essays is to develop the full Biblical contours of the fool.

THE FOOL IN WESTERN LITERATURE

Yet before we plunge into the Biblical world of the fool, it might be helpful to look at how the fool has functioned literarily in our tradition in the last millennium or so. He has had a rather difficult history, a history that has ventured rather far from the world of Proverbs. The *Oxford English Dictionary* tells us that the word fool is ultimately derived from the Latin "follem," which meant "bellows" and, in late medieval Latin, a "windbag" or "empty-headed person." By the time of the Middle Ages, the concept of fool, so carefully delineated in Proverbs had been shorn of its negative moral connotations. In fact, the OED tells us that the current usage of "fool" has a much stronger meaning than it did a millennium ago.

The major reason for the semantic shift from fool as bad person to fool as windbag or dunce emerged from the medieval festival called the Feast of Fools, or *festa stultorum*.[1] At the heart of this comic dramatic presentation was the upending of social conventions by young actors who gave mock presentations of the roles of "great" people. So, for example, the pope or a bishop might be ridiculed by a young person's clumsy presentation of this noble personage. Though condemned by leading churchmen

---

1   http://en.wikipedia.org/wiki/Feast_of_Fools

and even forbidden by the Council of Basel in 1431, the idea of a ludicrous presentation of a noble person became deeply engrained in the European psyche.

Though not genetically related to Feast of Fools, the appearance of the fool in Elizabethan literature, most familiarly in Shakespeare, seared the idea of the fool into the consciousness of the West. Who can forget the clever Touchstone of *As You Like It*? Or, perhaps alluding directly to the medieval "festa," Feste of *Twelfth Night*? Some have called Shakespeare's presentation of the unnamed fool in *King Lear* the most memorable of all. In Shakespeare's day (early 17th century), the fool functioned as entertainment for the royal household, but could be widely different in literary presentation. He could be a simple person, gullible, almost a bit retarded, easily exploited. Again, he could be a misshapen individual, like a hunchback or dwarf, kept around much as one would keep a pet. Finally, and most powerfully in *King Lear*, he could have a highly developed wit, intellect and quickness in repartee, a quickness which could lift the spirits, excite laughter, take the sovereign's mind off the cares he faced in ruling the kingdom and even not so subtly criticize the monarch. In this latter role, the fool could "speak truth to power," but he would do so in such manner that no one would take him actually to be undermining the king.

A striking example is in Act I of King Lear. Lear has just called the fool a "bitter fool." The fool then makes a distinction between the "bitter" and "sweet" fool. He says:

> "That lord that counseled thee
> To give away thy land,
> Come place him here by me;
> Do though for him stand.

The sweet and bitter fool
Will presently appear:
The one in motley here,
The other found out—there." I.4.138-145.

Lear gets the drift of what he is saying, "Dost thou call me fool, boy?" To which the fool responds,

"All thy other titles thou has given away;
that thou was born with." I.4.146-148.[2]

But the fool gradually disappeared in Western literature. More than one scholar has argued that in order to have the fool you have to have royalty, and a sort of sacramental, or at least whimsical view of the world—a world which many saw as dying with the French Enlightenment and the rise of modern science.[3] Now we are controlled by the spirit of science and rational inquiry. Apart from editorial cartoons, most criticism of elected officials comes through pointed criticism, finely developed essays, or even personal invective. The fool, in his Shakespearean sense, has seemed to perish along with that Elizabethan world.

Yet, he still tries to show himself every once in a while. The amusing and sad short story by Isaac Bashevis Singer, *Gimpel the Fool*, tells the story of what in Yiddish is known as a "poor schlemiel."[4] Gimpel is a simple person, the first type of the Shakespearean fool mentioned above, who is constantly being taken in by his neighbors. Someone tells him that his (dead) parents have risen from the grave; Gimpel goes running

2   Quoted in Peter J. Leithart, *Deep Comedy* (2006), p. 134.
3   A helpful discussion is here: http://wpl.lib.in.us/roger/FOOL.html
4   A summary of this delightful story is here: http://www.answers.com/topic/gimpel-the-fool-story-2.

out of his shop to see if this is the case. He eventually marries a wife, but she mercilessly cuckolds him, denying it even when he catches her *in flagrante*. There really is no "moral" to the story; Gimpel just ends up dreaming of a time and place where there is no deception or chicanery.

I would argue that the characterization of Forrest Gump in the blockbuster 1994 movie so named is meant to remind us of the fool. He isn't a fool because he is misshapen; indeed, he was able to perform some impressive athletic feats. He is a very simple person, and his simplicity allows for him to utter all kinds of homespun wisdom quotable by people well after the movie. He was loyal to a fault, overlooking obvious drawbacks in other people because he always believed in the goodness of people. If every fool were as entertaining as Forrest Gump, the world would be a kinder, gentler place.

CONCLUSION—ON TO PROVERBS

So, the fool lives today or, to say it more precisely, a type of the Shakespearean fool still lives. There still will be room for his characterization, but it takes quite a literary or cinematographic imagination to pull it off. My point in this section, however, is that another type of fool needs to be rehabilitated—the fool in Proverbs. We don't need to bring him back because we want to admire him or even hold him up to ridicule. The fool in Proverbs needs recapturing because he is a type of person we meet in the world, and a type of person whom we have to know how to handle. To put it differently, if we *don't* know how to encounter the fool, we stand the risk of being sucked into his machinations, of being emptied of our emotional energy, of being thought fools ourselves. I believe that one of the keys to a revitalized national and international community in our day is the ability to recognize, avoid and isolate the fool from our public discourse. They, like Jesus' poor, will probably always be with us. Just because they are present, however, doesn't mean that we should give them the keys to the city.

Thus, my exposition of the fool in the Book of Proverbs has a most serious end; it is to empower us to recognize and wisely handle foolishness wherever we find it, so that wisdom, and not folly, will have the last word in our public and private lives. In order to do this, we need not only delineate the contours of the fool, but we have to meet also several people that are his allies: the gullible, the mocker or scoffer and the lazy person. Each needs to be given his due, even though we do best not to give him more than that.

Day Ten

THE FOOL IN FULL

IN THE PREVIOUS ESSAY I introduced us ever so briefly to the fool in Proverbs before following his trail through our literary tradition. In this essay I will draw the major contours of the fool's character in Proverbs before focusing on one of his more objectionable traits—his quick temper and inappropriate speech. Careful attention to the wide-ranging character of the fool in Proverbs, as well as his particular traits, convinces me that his portrayal in Proverbs is even more memorable and telling than the fool in Shakespeare.

GENERAL CHARACTERIZATION OF THE FOOL IN PROVERBS

I introduced the fool colorfully in the last essay by giving "nine B's" that characterize him. The fool "blusters, blunders, bludgeons, bloviates, blisters, blabs, blets, babbles and bursts."[1]

1 I will use "he" or "she" indiscriminately to describe the fool. It seems that foolishness isn't primarily nested in one gender.

We need to draw his character more carefully now. The fool's basic identity is rooted in impatience. She can't stand to be corrected. She can't stand to let another person finish his or her thoughts. She can't bear to hold back her reaction to what is going on before her. But the dangerous thing about the fool is that when she reacts prematurely she explodes in anger. When she does this, she shows that she despises advice. She not only affects herself by this action but manages to bring others down, too. She tends to incite dissatisfaction, exploiting uncertainty and fear, which causes others to react to her in the same way she is reacting to a situation. Sooner or later, all are drawn into her net, and general chaos ensues. Sometimes the fool actually desires this chaos; sometimes she doesn't seem to know exactly what she is doing; other times she acts from such arrogance and unconcern for others that no one can influence her. In short, for Proverbs, the fool is not simply an amusing expression of humanity gone astray; she is a dangerous person who threatens the safety and stability of a community.

A few verses will illustrate the perniciousness of the fool's behavior and speech for the author of Proverbs.

"A fool takes no pleasure in understanding,
but only in expressing personal opinion," 18:2.

Do you know people like this? They can hardly *wait* for you to finish saying your piece, and then they burst forth with their words, words that show no awareness that you have just spoken. One friend told me that in a conversation she had with another, the other person asked my friend's name *four times* — and *still* couldn't remember it. The Biblical language of "gushing" or "bursting forth" is used to describe the fool:

"One who is clever conceals knowledge,
>
> but the mind of a fool broadcasts folly," 12:23.

"A fool gives full vent to anger,
>
> but the wise quietly holds it back," 29:11.

"The tongue of the wise dispenses knowledge
>
> but the mouths of fools pour out folly," 15:2.

If we come upon a person who is "venting," we tend to think one of two things: (1) this person *really* has a grievance; or (2) this person is just *out of control*. The fool is one who continually pours out his vitriol, and it doesn't take long to realize that he has no self-control.

And the venom is real. It is meant to provoke a quarrel.

"It is honorable to refrain from strife,
>
> but every fool is quick to quarrel," 20:3.

Lest we miss it:

"A fool's lips bring strife,
>
> and a fool's mouth invites a flogging," 18:6.

When you spend some time thinking about communication, you understand how easy it is for miscommunication to develop and strife to ensue. Miscommunication can arise through imprecise words, unclear thinking, overcharged rhetoric, irascible temperament, or simply from lack of attentiveness of one or all parties to the encounter. In fact, it is very difficult to make good communication happen. The fool can't do it for the following reason:

> "The discerning person looks to wisdom,
>> but the fool to the ends of the earth," 17:24.

The fool is distracted, looking at other things, bigger goals, world-wide impact, and is thus unable to be attentive to a matter (cf. 16:20).

But the fool is much more (or much less!) than this. He speaks before thinking and provokes or prolongs quarrels, but he also has other unattractive traits. He regularly exercises poor judgment. He does so because he neither seeks out nor listens to counsel. Characteristic of the wise in Proverbs is the fact that they seek and give heed to advice. Counsel is prized by the wise, but not by the fool.

> "Fools think their own way is right,
>> but the wise listen to advice," 12:15.

One of the reasons fools can't listen to advice is that they arrogantly think there is one truth in a situation and that they have the right way to this truth. Fools exalt themselves (cf. 30:32) and are wise in their own eyes (cf. 26:12). They don't believe there is any reason to seek advice because they, unlike the rest of us poor slobs, don't really need any help. Indeed, they despise counsel, and they can't really stand the correction by the wise. They bristle at it and either ignore it or lash out at the one doing the correcting. Little do they know that their way is the way of death (14:12).

112

REACTIONS TO THE FOOL

Is the fool educable? Can he be argued out of folly? Convinced to turn away from his folly? Proverbs never gives us a definitive answer to that question, but it is skeptical. The only verses that give hope for the fool is one like 29:20,

> "Do you see someone hasty in speech?
>> There is more hope for a fool than for anyone
>> like that."

This doesn't exactly express hope for the fool; it does suggest, however, that there may be ways for the fool to change. Yet, the fool really has no interest in changing. He doesn't think he has any reason to change, and so therefore any hope that he will do so voluntarily is misplaced.

It is in this context that Proverbs expresses some of its strongest vituperative rancor towards and scorn of the fool.

> "Better to meet a she-bear robbed of its cubs
>> than to confront a fool immersed in folly," 17:12.

> "Crush a fool in a mortar with a pestle, along with
>> crushed grain,
>> but the folly will not be driven out," 27:22.

It is because of this approach to the fool that we can understand the sadness and hopelessness of the following:

"The one who begets a fool gets trouble;
　　the parent of a fool has no joy," 17:21.

Or the seeming finality of these verses:

"The lips of the righteous feed many,
　　but fools die for lack of sense," 10:21.

"The mouths of fool are their ruin,
　　and their lips a snare to themselves," 18:7.

Does this describe this anyone you know? It wasn't until I read and studied Proverbs closely that I recognized in the discussion of the fool some people with whom I was dealing in my professional life. They had stymied me, angered me, distracted me and frustrated me. But once I read the Book of Proverbs, I not only began to understand them but, in all instances, I was subsequently able to evade their venom and isolate their rage. The wisdom of Proverbs brings light to our path today.

A WORD ON THE FOOL'S SPEECH

We understand the fool more precisely when we see the rapidity and vehemence of his inappropriate speech. Wise people are characterized by their ability to "ponder" a situation (15:28), while the fool can't restrain his emotions and verbal response. Let's begin with 12:16,

"Fools show their anger at once,
　　but the prudent ignore an insult."

The Hebrew in the first colon stops us in our tracks. The

word translated "at once" is *bayom*. Literally it says that fools make known their anger "in a day," i.e., the same day that a situation is presented to them. They have no capacity for reflective consideration of a problem. *That* indeed is what makes them a fool.

Indeed, the most vivid word used for the fool's immediate reaction is that he "gushes." While the tongue of the wise dispenses knowledge, "the mouths of fools pour out folly" (15:2). The image behind the "gushing out" or "pouring out" is of a fountain or stream that spews forth its water. Just as looking in one's reflection in water provided the context for one of our essays (see exposition on 27:19), so the reality of gushing water provides another. Gushing water is even more forceful than the Biblical notion of "living water." In a land where water is scarce, any reference to "gushing" or "pouring forth" ought to be noted.

So powerful is the image of this kind of stream for the author of Proverbs that both wisdom and folly can be said to "gush" forth. The basic verse showing that this is a characteristic of wisdom is 18:4,

> "The words of the mouth are deep waters;
>> the fountain of wisdom is a gushing stream."

When wisdom calls forth to the simple, it did so with strongly flowing words. Let's hear the entire context:

> "How long, O simple ones, will you love being simple?
> How long will scoffers delight in their scoffing
>> And fools hate knowledge?
> Give heed to my reproof.
> I will pour out my thoughts to you," 1:22-23.

The verb translated "pour forth" or "pour out" is *nagah*, and it appears 10 other times in the Bible. It can sometimes be used of arrogant people:

> "They pour out (*nagah*) their arrogant words;
>> all the evildoers boast," Psalm 94:4.

But usually it relates to copious expressions of positive emotion, wisdom, teaching or joy. Most memorable is its use in Psalm 19 to describe the overabundant glory of the heavenly handiwork of God. You can almost heard Franz Josef Haydn in the background:

> "The heavens are telling the glory of God;
>> and the firmament proclaims his handiwork.
> Day to day pours forth (*nagah*) speech," 19:1-2.

Or, in the longest Psalm of the Bible, celebrating the divine law, the writer says:

> "My lips will pour forth (*nagah*) praise,
>> because you teach me your statutes," 119:171.

The fool in Proverbs gushes forth his folly. In one other passage, it is the "mouth of the wicked" which pours out evil (15:28). Proverbs never explicitly ties the fool to the wicked, but the linguistic leap isn't too far. The fool gets angry the "same day" he is provoked; and the expression of his anger can best be described as an "eruption" or "effusion" or "powerfully issuing forth."

When the fool rages, he is not only expressing anger, as if anger is a subsistent entity separate from the person. He is, as it were, *becoming* anger. That is how we should read the subtle Hebrew of 29:11. The NRSV translates the first colon:

"A fool gives full vent to anger."

But the Hebrew is "the fool gives full vent to his spirit." The last word is the usual word in Hebrew for the human, and divine, spirit (*ruah*) or wind. Thus, it is a word representing the full scope of vitality. It is the "spirit" in a person that is important, not the age, says Elihu (Job 32: 18; 33:4). Thus, a fool's anger, venom, quick response, impatient words, shrill tone, uncomfortable demeanor, is really an expression of his essential vitality or energy or being. That is why you can beat him in a mortar with a pestle, and the folly won't leave him (22:27).

Waltke quotes a fitting rabbinic word to close our chapter. In Tractate Eruvim, a tractate of the Order Moed of the Babylonian Talmud, one recognizes a person from three things: his cup (*kos*), his purse *(kis)* and his annoyance *(ka'as)*.[2] This means that, for the rabbis, a person's essential character was demonstrated in how she behaved while eating, while dealing with money and while dealing with distraction or conflict. The fool simply cannot handle the last one with equanimity. He thereby makes life unendurable for all around him. Or, giving the Book of Proverbs the last word:

"A stone is heavy, and sand is weighty,
    but a fool's provocation is heavier than both," 27:3.

---

2   *The Book of Proverbs, 1-15*, p. 534.

Day Eleven

MOR(E) ON THE FOOL—A FOLLIED MISCELLANY

THE BASIC THESIS of my last essay was that the fool in Proverbs lacks patience. From that lack flows all sorts of harmful characteristics—he quickly loses his temper ("on the same day"), he starts quarrels, he is inattentive, he is impervious to discipline, he despises the wise, he is arrogant and, generally, he erodes whatever fabric of community exists among people. If everything the legendary King Midas touched turned to gold, everything the fool touches becomes tarnished with ineradicable stains.

But there is more. In this chapter I will briefly describe some more traits of the fool, then call attention to a few passages in Proverbs regarding the impropriety of granting the fool a position of trust, and then finish with what I call the great paradox of the fool, or how to deal with a fool who is standing right in front of you making foolish claims about something.

119

A FEW MORE WORDS ON THE FOOL

Two additional characteristics of the fool, which amplify the last chapter, are that the fool is *rash* and the fool *rants*. The verse which takes us to his rashness is 12:18:

"Rash words are like sword thrusts,
但 but the tongue of the wise brings healing."

Since the "rash words" come in the immediate context of the fool who gets angry "on the same day" (12:16), we can assume that the fool is the one who utters the rash words. The word translated "rash" (it is the verb *batah*) is rare in the Old Testament—occurring only four times. Yet it links us with the tradition of a rash act of Moses which fills out the concept nicely. From Ps. 106,

"They angered the Lord at the waters of Meribah,
and it went ill with Moses on their account;
for they made his spirit bitter,
and he spoke words that were rash,"
(*bateh*), vv. 32-33.

The event to which this Psalm points is Moses' upbraiding of the people of Israel for complaining about the ability of God to deliver them from the predicament of lack of water (Ex. 14:14-17; Num. 20:8-12). In the story in Numbers, Moses is commanded to rebuke the people. He not only does so, in harsher language than expected, but he strikes the rock from which pure water would flow. In short, Moses let the people of Israel "get under his skin." He reacted to their challenge with immediate anger and petulance. He struck the rock as a sign of his authority and control. In a word, he acted rashly.

The fool also acts rashly. He speaks too quickly and with unnecessary vehemence. Another proverb points out a rash activity which, though not explicitly tied to the fool's behavior, is fully consistent with it.

> "It is a snare for one to say rashly, 'It is holy,'
> and begin to reflect only after making a vow,"
>
> 20:25.

That verse says it perfectly. A fool is one who makes commitments, promises, vows, interpretations on the spur of the moment, all the while not realizing that his words have immured him in a prison of difficulties. He makes commitments and then wants to back out on them a moment after everyone else has changed *their* schedules to accommodate him.

Because rashness is at the heart of a fool's activity, one can understand the cautionary words of 30:21-22:

> "Under three things the earth trembles;
>   under four things it cannot bear up:
> a slave when he becomes king,
>   and a fool when glutted with food."

Once the fool has filled his stomach, it is as if he feels invincible. He feels free to continue acting rashly, without consideration of the danger to which he is exposing himself or others. He doesn't know that the way he is following is the way of death (14:12) or that he will die because of lack of sense (10:21). Yet, in the process, his out-of-control manner damages and destroys others.

In brief, the fool lacks self-control. Proverbs has two precious verses about self-control, which are so clear in their meaning but so radical in their implications that we barely can believe they are true.

> "One who is slow to anger is better than the mighty,
>   and one whose temper is controlled than one
>   who captures a city," 16:32.

> "Like a city breached, without walls,
>   is one who lacks self-control," 25:28.

That's all there is to it. Control your temper and you are "better than the mighty." Shouldn't *everyone* be taking "anger management" classes to learn the secret of this kind of equanimity?

The fool also *rants*. Since I broached his anger so fully in the last essay, all I will say here is that while the anger seems to be something that comes on the fool immediately, the *rant* is his *continual* angry, bombastic activity.

> "If the wise go to law with fools,
>   there is ranting and ridicule without relief," 29:9.

WHAT IS INAPPROPRIATE FOR THE FOOL

The Book of Proverbs has a deep sense of what one might call the "fitting" or "appropriate" or "right" thing to do in life. Such a view arises from another picture out of the world of Proverbs — the balance or scale. Unjust balances are an abomination to the

Lord (11:1; 20:10, 23). The just balance stands for a concept of justice, rightness, appropriateness, or fittingness that underlies the moral universe of Proverbs. A few other verses show it:

"To impose a fine on the innocent is not right,
or to flog the noble for their integrity," 17:26.

"It is not right to be partial to the guilty,
or to subvert the innocent in judgment," 18:5.

Thus, in the mind of the author/compiler of Proverbs, certain things are just not "right." A more colorful way of saying this is expressed in the "three/four" Proverb of 30:21-22. The world trembles under three things, and under four it "cannot bear up." The world just can't endure certain things.

One of the things that is not right or appropriate or which the world can't endure is the fool in certain relationships in life. Three verses illustrate this:

"Fine speech is not becoming to a fool;
still less is false speech to a ruler," 17:7.

"It is not fitting for a fool to live in luxury,
much less for a slave to rule over princes," 19:10.

"Like snow in summer or rain in harvest,
so honor is not fitting to a fool," 26:1.

The reason that a fool shouldn't live in luxury is that he thereby will be able to stuff his face (30:22) and have more security to rant, get angry and upset the community. The reason a fool shouldn't be honored is that he will think that everyone is affirming his brilliance, and he will let his arrogance further carry him away to do more destructive activity. The reason a fool shouldn't use fine speech is that it just doesn't "fit" her character. A word "fitly" spoken is like "apples of gold in a setting of silver" (25:11). This kind of speaking takes a lot of training and is the prerogative of the wise.

Thus, don't give the fool honor. Don't reward them with luxury. Don't expect wise things to come from their mouths. Indeed, all who make use of the fool will regret it.

> "It is like binding a stone in a sling
>   to give honor to a fool.
> Like a thornbush brandished by the hand of a
>   drunkard
>   is a proverb in the mouth of a fool.
> Like an archer who wounds everybody
>   is one who hires a passing fool or drunkard," 26:8-10.

The fool is a lethal person with whom to deal. She is like an unpredictable person armed with a dangerous weapon.

ANSWERING THE FOOL

So, how do you deal with such a person? The question is neither academic or abstruse. Whoever has had a life of public service and engagement, or has been in leadership in any enterprise, knows that a good deal of their time is taken up dealing with fools. But you often can't simply dismiss or fire a fool. There are repercussions, both legal and practical, that may ensue. You have to "negotiate" the fool, deal carefully with him or her, and try your best to isolate him and contain his rage and dangerous tendencies. It takes all of the patience and skill that a wise person can muster.

I will have more to say about this when we look at how to deal with other foolish-type people (fools, the lazy, mockers), but for the remainder of the chapter I will reflect on a paradox of dealing with the fool. The paradox is placed right in our field of vision by two apparently contradictory verses that appear next to each other. They read:

> "Do not answer fools according to their folly,
>   Or you will be a fool yourself.
> Answer fools according to their folly,
>   Or they will be wise in their own eyes," 26:4-5.

The paradox leaps out at us. We are, apparently at the same time, *not* to answer the fool and *to answer* the fool. Which will it be? The grammatical construction in Hebrew is identical. The word "according to" translates the same Hebrew preposition (*ke*). Nothing more can be said about *ke* other than it means "in agreement in kind."[1] How can we both answer and not answer the fool in ways that deal with his folly? Is the Book of Proverbs being helpful here or are we just being taken through a maze of contradictory statements until confusion ensues?

A way through the maze emerges when we recognize how the Septuagint, the Greek translation of the OT made in the last few centuries before Christ, rendered the preposition *ke* differently in each verse. In 26:4 the Greek has the word *pros* and in 26:5, we have *kata*. Indeed, these Greek prepositions

---

1   Bruce Waltke, *The Book of Proverbs, Chapters 16-31*, p. 349.

each have a rather wide semantic field, but the general sense of the *pros* is "in agreement with" or "facing towards," while *kata* means "against," in addition to "according to."

Let's see where these renderings may take us. If we answer a fool *pros* his folly, we are answering in a way that is consistent with, agrees with, or is similar in style to the fool. It would, in our language, be a sort of "tit for tat" response. The fool abuses, and we abuse in return; the fool criticizes, and we immediately return the criticism. And the result is that we become fools ourselves. The Hebrew is vivid. We become fools, "even you!" Fancy that. By so responding to the fool, we have entered into his world of quick retaliation, instead of "pondering" (15:28) the matter or letting the Lord (20:22) deal with the issue.

This interpretation would require quite an exposition to relate it to the variety of life circumstances where we might respond to verbal provocation. What might this verse mean, if anything, when we are engaged in a debate, for example, or a disagreement in a public gathering? No easy answer is available. The reason? Because of 26:5. We are also, at the same time as we are warily *not* answering the fool in 26:4, *answering* the fool. We need to answer the fool *kata* his folly, lest she seem wise in her own eyes. This suggests we answer a fool *against* or *distinctly from* or *in a manner different from* the way she speaks. Rather than letting the fool declare the terms and scope of discussion, forcing us thereby into a sort of retaliatory response, we need to reframe the discussion or, at least, not get sucked into the way of speaking demanded by the fool. The fool may give us a "yes or no" alternative; the wise person learns to puncture the security of that adversative by answering in another way.

We engage the fool *kata* her folly because it isn't good, fitting or right to let the fool's foolishness go unchallenged. It may do no good for the fool to hear herself upbraided or disproven, but it does a world of good for the onlookers.

CONCLUSION

Proverbs doesn't let us off the hook in dealing with the fool. We can't simply say, "You're fired!" and expect the fool meekly to go away. We have to deal with her. By weighing our response, pondering how to answer, and then responding *kata* the fool, we can affirm the path of wisdom and marginalize the predacious and malicious activity of the fool.

Day Twelve

FILLING OUT THE FOOLS GALLERY-THE SCOFFER AND THE SLUGGARD

THOUGH "THE FOOL" is the primary category of person standing in opposition to "the wise," she is not the only one who can be so characterized. The two most prominent other subtypes of the wisdom-averse in Proverbs are the mocker/scoffer and the sluggard/lazybones. Just as the American Elm (*Ulmus americana*) is the most noteworthy exemplar of the *Ulmus* genus of trees, though the Homestead Elm (*Ulmus* 'Homestead') and the striking Lacebark Elm[1] are more specific and rare exemplars, so the Fool is our "genus" category, with species of the fool being these two unfortunate types of people.

Several features of the mocker and the sluggard are noteworthy; each has one trait that is his Achilles heel. The mocker (*les* in Hebrew) is possessed by such insolence and

---

1   A picture of the exfoliating bark of the Lacebark Elm (*Ulmus parviflora*) is here. http://www.hort.uconn.edu/plants/help/barktex/ulmpar.jpg.

arrogance that he lives aggressively and almost violently. He, along with the fool, shares the unattractive trait of pride, but the mocker seemingly is so driven by pride that it actually defines his character. The sluggard or lazy person (*atsel* in Hebrew) is characterized by unfulfilled craving or coveting. Because she can't have her cravings realized, she never can quite get around to any productive activity in life. While the mocker is actually a dangerous person, a firebrand who always seems to feed a fire with more fuel, the lazy person is a sort of object of amazement and disbelief as she whiles her life away. The mocker tries to destroy another's soul, but the lazybones wastes her own. Let's consider each in turn.

MEETING THE MOCKER

The first time we meet the mocker or scoffer in Proverbs is in connection with the fool. Wisdom cries out to them:

> "How long, O simple ones, will you love being
>   simple?
> How long will scoffers delight in their scoffing
>   and fools hate knowledge?" 1:22

Scoffers take delight in scoffing. Which is probably to be expected. But the key to the scoffer's heart is his arrogance. Note the piling up of terms in 21:24,

> "The proud, haughty person, named 'Scoffer,'
>   acts with arrogant pride."

It would have been enough to say that the *les* is proud or

is haughty, but the author not only heaps up the adjectives but also connects the scoffer with yet another phrase—"acts with arrogant pride."

Particularly to be noted is the word translated "arrogant" (*zedon*). It probably is better rendered "insolent," and it, along with the noun *zed* (insolence), appears about 30 times in the Bible. While many of its usages simply describe people who are the Psalmist's enemy (7X in Ps. 119 alone), three usages illumine the context of Proverbs 21:24. In all three, insolence is manifest in opposing the clear word or the authorities appointed by God. For example, we have:

> "If a prophet speaks in the name of the Lord but
> the thing does not take place or prove true, it is a
> word that the Lord has not spoken. The prophet
> has spoken it presumptuously (*zedon*); do not be
> frightened by it," Deut. 18:22.

> "As for anyone who presumes to disobey (lit. "acts
> with *zedon*) the priest appointed to minister there to
> the Lord your God, or the judge, that person shall
> die. All the people will hear and be afraid, and will
> not act presumptuously again," Deut. 17:12-13.

When Jeremiah had spoken the Word of God to the people in exile, a word which they didn't want to hear, a deputation of men came to him to upbraid him. The text calls them the "insolent men" (*zedon*), and their first words to Jeremiah were, "You are telling a lie," Jer. 43:1-2.

We can infer from the rich usage of *zedon* in the Scriptures that the scoffer or mocker is one who not simply "acts arrogantly," as we might say, but basically cannot accept the authority even of the Word of God or of the duly appointed authorities in the community. In short, no one, *no one* has any authority for the mocker. He is his own authority.

We ought to pause for a moment on this point because this trait is the key to understanding the mocker. He is an authority unto himself. Proverbs never speculates as to where this sense comes from, but the fact is that the scoffer listens to no one, can take correction from no one, and can hear nothing other than the insistent cries of his own mind. Waltke points out that Prov. 21:24 appears in the context of other proverbs that talk about attacking a city (21:22) and guarding and watching things (21:23), and so he suggests that the repeated and forceful language describing the scoffer in 21:24 as it were invests the scoffer with a warlike or violent tendency.[2] The mocker's arrogance is an aggressive, self-assertive, pushy arrogance. The mocker is "in your face" and doesn't mind being there, even when he is dead wrong.

As a result of this activity, he "seeks wisdom in vain," 14:6. The Hebrew phrase is a telling one. The first three words of 14:6 are the traditional words for searching out wisdom. "Seeks the mocker wisdom," it says. But then, we are brought up short by the little Hebrew word *vaayin*, "and it is not" or "he has not." It is as if the scoffer takes all the pains to search for wisdom as the one in Prov. 2 who is encouraged to seek it, but here "he has not." He can't get it. Instead of a full cup, "a scorching wind" will be his portion (cf. Ps. 11:6).

Why can't the scoffer get wisdom? Because he, like the fool of which he is a subset, has "no mind to learn," 17:16. He has no mind to learn because he is lacking that central characteristic of the learner—a desire for, and a willingness to accept, correction.

---

2   Bruce Waltke, *The Book of Proverbs, 15-31*, pp. 186-87.

Learning requires humility, a sense that something and someone apart from yourself has lessons to teach you. In order to learn, you have to still the raging voices of your heart and listen to the messages that come to you by words, deeds, pictures, and examples. But hear how the scoffer relates to instruction or discipline.

> "A wise child loves discipline,
>> but a scoffer does not listen to rebuke," 13:1.

> "Scoffers do not like to be rebuked,
>> they will not go to the wise," 15:12.

Indeed, in a theme to be developed later in this book, the wise differ from the mocker or scoffer in many ways, one of which is how one responds to correction.

> "Whoever corrects a scoffer wins abuse;
>> whoever rebukes the wicked gets hurt.
> A scoffer who is rebuked will only hate you;
>> The wise, when rebuked, will love you," 9:7-8.

Ultimately, the violent and pushy arrogance of the scoffer will tear down the community.

> "Scoffers set a city aflame,
> but the wise turn away wrath," 29:8.

That is why Proverbs uses the strongest language it can to denounce the scoffer:

"The devising of folly is sin;
 and the scoffer is an abomination to all," 24:9.

These people still live today, and they inhabit almost every cranny of business, education, the human services and government. They must be dealt with effectively if you are to make any progress at all in your work and life. The next essay tells us how to handle them.

INTRODUCING THE SLUGGARD/LAZYBONES

One of the most memorable descriptions of any person in Proverbs is of the sluggard in 26:13-16. Note the vividness and hilarity of the picture.

"The lazy person says, 'There is a lion in the road!
     There is a lion in the streets!"
 As a door turns on its hinges,
     So does a lazy person in bed.
 The lazy person buries a hand in the dish,
     And is too tired to bring it back to the mouth.
 The lazy person is wiser in self-esteem
     Than seven who can answer discreetly."

These verses skillfully explore the psychology of the lazy person. The lazy person has to give a reason for her inactivity. It is an unlikely excuse — a lion in the streets. Just so that you would know, there were no known lions roaming Israelite urban centers in the first millennium BCE. The equivalent might be, "I can't go outside. I might catch swine flu!" Or, "I can't go to work; I might be run over by a truck." Though each is mathematically possible, they form an improbable basis on which to base inactivity.

We then follow the lazy person into her world of inertness. The next "picture" we see is of her lounging on the bed. She turns restlessly as the door turns on its hinges. Maybe she squeaks, too, squealing that she is uncomfortable or that she is being put-upon in some way. But there is more. We then see the lazy person eating. Perhaps she has marshaled the strength to get herself out of bed; perhaps the bowl with the food lies within reach so she doesn't even have to rise to eat. But, all of this is rather academic for the lazy person, since she puts her hand in the food dish but doesn't even have the strength or ambition to bring it to her mouth. In short, the lazy person has given up on life because she can't even do the basic things necessary to make life productive (rise and, figuratively speaking, get out of the house). As a result, she doesn't "plow in season," 20:4. She is instructed to visit the ant and see a real example of industriousness, 6:6-11, but since she doesn't seem to want to rise from bed, it is unlikely that she will take the salutary advice in that passage. The end result is a way that is "overgrown with thorns" (15:19), while the "path of the upright is a level highway."

The lazy person's indolence, sluggishness, passiveness and quiescence is rooted, paradoxically enough, in craving. In two instances the word for craving or coveting is used to describe her. Let's look at each.

> "The craving of the lazy person is fatal,
> for lazy hands refuse to labor," 21:25.

> "The appetite of the lazy craves, and gets nothing,
> while the appetite of the diligent is richly
> supplied," 13:4.

The verb *awah* appears about 20 times in the Bible and is normally translated "desire," "crave," or "covet." In its four other occurrences in Proverbs (21:26; 23:3, 6; 24:1) it refers to unhealthy and harmful cravings, such as the impropriety of craving the king's delicacies (23:3) or desiring to be in the presence of the wicked (24:1). Two instances of its use outside of Proverbs express an extreme state of longing and desire. Here they are:

> "Hear, O daughter, consider and incline your ear;
> forget your people and your father's house,
> and the king will desire your beauty," Ps. 45:10-11.

Then, when David was mightily thirsty, holed up in his stronghold to ward off the attack of the Philistines, the text has:

> "David said longingly, 'O that someone would give
> me water to drink from the well of Bethlehem that is
> by the gate!" II Sam. 23:15.

The craving thus envisioned in Proverbs 13:4 can be interpreted in the light of the II Samuel passage. The lazy person can't get out of bed, can't even reach into the dish to eat, because she is *craving* all the time. She doesn't crave work and diligence and the things that the wise know make for a rich life; she craves, perhaps, the *vision* of herself in success or honor or ease. All she can see is the "victory" down the line, the time when everything is given her on a silver plate. So strong is the mental picture of herself (she is "wise in her self-esteem—26:16), that she simply is unable to formulate a plan to accomplish anything in life.

136

There is, I fear, a significant section of the population which never really understands the connection between work and success, between effort and wisdom. It isn't really an obvious connection, since so many people who do so well *are* much more beautiful or athletic than the "average Jane." Thus, the lazy person thinks that their special skill, whatever it is, ought to be as seemingly effortless as Roger Federer burying a forehand or Heidi Klum walking down a runway. They just expect life "to happen."

But it won't. The starkest Biblical judgment on that way of thinking is in 13:4 itself. It says, "the soul (the word is *nephesh*, a richly-laden Biblical word) of the lazy one yearns." But then there is dropped into the text a word like in 14:6 above: *vaayin*, "and it is not," or "and she is not." She is full of longing and craving, but there is nothing ultimately to show for it. Nothing at all.

Day Thirteen

GANDERING AT THE GULLIBLE;
RESPONDING TO ALL

I HAVE AVOIDED talking about one category of people until now because of their rather ambiguous position in Proverbs. They are important in the flow of Proverbs, but they are not easily categorized with the fools or the wise. These are the gullible or the simple (*peti*). The word *peti* occurs 14 times in Proverbs and only four times in the rest of the Bible; thus, we see that this is a special category of people "invented" or "discovered" by Proverbs to illustrate a point about human nature.

The best way to characterize the *peti* is as "fools in training" or "potential fools." They are normally thought of as young people who are inexperienced in the ways of the world and thus easily affected by competing and contrasting claims, but the word could also apply to anyone inexperienced in a matter. I am a sort of *peti* with respect to matters of technology; I tend to believe anyone's explanation of a computer problem, as long as they are under 22 years old.

THE FIVE FEATURES OF THE GULLIBLE

1. They Are Malleable

Five aspects of Proverbs' delineation of the *peti* are important to note. First, they are *malleable*. One of the purposes of Proverbs, stated in the preamble, is "to teach shrewdness to the simple," 1:4. Shrewdness is not defined here, but elsewhere it is associated with the clever who "do all things intelligently," 13:16. Thus, the purpose of teaching the *peti* is to lead them to be wise. There is hope for the *peti*.

2. They Are Vulnerable

Yet, don't get your hopes up too quickly. Second, as a result of their malleability, the *peti* are *vulnerable* or, in Proverbs' language, "without sense." The long narrative poem in Proverbs 7 probes this most helpfully. The hearer is exhorted, in familiar words, to "store up" the commandments of the teacher and to embrace wisdom as a "sister" and "intimate friend," 7:4. Then a story follows. The teacher has observed a familiar sight from his window. A simple person, a person without sense, is hanging around on the street. The "loose woman" approaches and invites him into her home. With much enticing speech she seduces him. The story is simply told:

> "Right away he follows her,
>   and goes like an ox to the slaughter," 7:22.

This story illustrates a larger competition for the soul of the *peti* that takes place on a daily basis. Proverbs 9 presents this competition in the language of dual appeals to the simple from

Lady Wisdom and Lady Folly. First, we hear from wisdom.

> "She has sent out her servant girls,
>> She calls from the highest places in the town,
> 'You that are simple, turn in here!'
>> To those without sense she says,
> 'Come, eat of my bread
>> and drink of the wine I have mixed.
> Lay aside immaturity (simpleness), and live,
>> and walk in the way of insight," 9:3-6.

But then, a few verses later, Lady Folly gets into the act. Note the way she appeals to the *peti,*

> "She sits at the door of her house,
>> on a seat at the high places of the town,
> calling to those who pass by,
>> who are going straight on their way,
> 'You who are simple, turn in here!'
>> And to those without sense she says,
> 'Stolen water is sweet,
>> and bread eaten in secret is pleasant," 9:13-17.

Folly's appeal is in the same words as wisdom's appeal, with one difference. Lady Folly *herself* is making it, while Wisdom sends her servant girls to make it. Why doesn't Wisdom *herself* show up to call upon the simple? Because, as we will see in the next section of the book, the wise are, generally, *hiding* themselves, or living in their own inscrutability. Wisdom needs a lot of time to cultivate and develop; one can't do so if one is out there "calling" all the time. So, unfortunately but truly, folly often dominates the airwaves; folly makes the personal appeal. Such an appeal is sometimes too alluring for the simple. They follow along and go into "the depths of Sheol," 9:18.

One way this problem is seen in our world today is in the way that competing ideologies vie for the attention of young people. In the 21st century this happens primarily through religious messages. Contrary to what the optimistic secularists were saying to us in the 1950s and 1960s, religion *isn't* dying in our world; its appeal seems to be more powerful than ever before.

A striking new book, by the young Muslim-American author Eboo Patel, explores the problem of faith for the world's young people.[1] Radical ideologies, whether Christian, Muslim, Hindu or other, give a young person a sense of identity, a way to define the world, a sense of empowerment amid the confusing welter of messages bombarding a person. The energy of young people, which loves to be thrown into things, is more easily captured by these radical ideologies because it gives such a clear task to people to perform, and promises incomparable rewards. The challenge for the future, as Patel sees it, is to build a passionate *moderate* movement in religion, one that truly celebrates and embraces the diversity of religious faiths in the world, but which embraces one's own faith in the midst of this diversity. The struggle for the soul of the 21st century will be a struggle of religions. Which voice will the simple, the *peti*, hear?

3. They Lack Good Judgment

Third, the *peti* don't have good judgment. The *peti* are not the same as the fool, who have *bad* judgment; they simply haven't had enough experience in life to be able to assess the

---

1   Eboo Patel, *Acts of Faith* (Beacon, 2008).

truth or likelihood of truth of messages coming to them. Thus, they are easily duped.

> "The simple believe everything,
>> but the clever consider their steps," 14:15.

There is a type of person whose belief system is formed by whomever he or she talks to last. The *peti* may fall into that category. The Epistle of James realizes the plasticity and gullibility of the simple; thus it warns not many of us to become teachers, "for we who teach will be judged with greater strictness," James 3:1. Greater strictness is applied to teachers because we are responsible not only for our own learning, but also, to a great degree, for that of our students.

4. They Will Pay For Their Choices

Fourth, the *peti* will pay the price for their simpleness, even though they are not yet fully responsible for their lives and choices. We know this to be true, though we sometimes chafe at the apparent injustice of this arrangement.

> "The clever see danger and hide,
>> but the simple go on, and suffer for it," 22:3.

Lest we miss the point, the verse is repeated at 27:13. One point about the Hebrew text is arresting. "Clever" is put in the singular while "simple" is put in the plural. Apparently there are a lot more of the latter than the former. The text doesn't tell us what the price is, though we know it quite well. It can be physical injury, emotional scarring, loss of money, loss of relationships, choices missed, benefits squandered. The simple don't know how to read the signs telling them to stop or hide or run.

5. They Have To Make A Choice

Finally, if the *peti* remain too long in their condition, they, as it were, turn into fools. Foolishness is the "default setting" on the "hardware" of personal identity. If you do nothing, you become a fool. Proverbs says it much more eloquently than I:

> "The simple are adorned with folly,
>> but the clever are crowned with knowledge," 14:18.

A better translation of the word rendered "are adorned with" is "inherit." The contrast in the verse is between two kinds of inheritance. That towards which the life of simplicity leads is folly. Therefore, the life of the *peti* is in the balance; his/her fate is undecided. But it won't be undecided for long. Now we understand the urgency of the exhortation in Proverbs 1-9 to "get wisdom" and "whatever else you get, get insight," 4:7.

WHAT TO DO WITH THESE PEOPLE?

It is clear that you educate the simple; you exhort them to choose the way of wisdom. There is still time for them to get wise, even if that time may be short. Whatever else they do in life, they need to "get wisdom."

But that isn't how the wise should relate to the fool, scoffer and lazybones. You are to drive out the scoffer (22:10) and give a rod to the back of the fool (10:13; 26:3) before leaving his presence (14:7). Because the lazybones doesn't tear apart the fabric of the community as the other two do, nothing is said about leaving them or driving them out. They simply are exhorted to go to the ant and learn its ways (6:6-11). Maybe all hope hasn't perished for them. The remainder of this essay focuses on dealing with the fool and the mocker/scoffer.

The most vehement words are reserved for the mocker/scoffer:

"Drive out a scoffer, and strife goes out;
quarreling and abuse will cease," 22:10.

The verb translated "drive out" (*garish*) is especially powerful in Hebrew. Of the many instances in which it is used, three are noteworthy:

"God drove out (*garash*) the man (from the garden
of Eden); and at the east of the garden of Eden
he placed the cherubim, and a sword flaming and
turning to guard the way to the tree of life,"
Gen. 3:24.

Then, after Cain killed his brother Abel and God condemned Cain to be a fugitive and a wanderer on the earth, Cain said:

"Today you have driven me (*garash*) away from the
soil, and I shall be hidden from your face...," Gen.
4:14.

Again, when God promised to bring the people of Israel into the Holy land, God also promised to clear the land for them.

"Little by little I will drive them out (*garash*) before
    you," Ex. 23:30.

These examples show that *garash* is used to express a
forceful, decisive and, in these cases, divine expulsion of people
from a situation. Such should be the decisiveness attendant the
expulsion of the mocker from the wise.

Why? Because the mocker as shown himself unable to
live in community. He delights to tear it down. He sets it aflame
(29:8). He cannot take correction. Indeed, "Whoever corrects a
scoffer wins abuse," 9:7. The mocker is unable to learn, and in
order to keep him from tearing out the heart of the community,
he must not only be opposed; he must be removed. I can testify
that when you have such a person "on your committee" or "in
your community," you simply have to get rid of the person if
you want to get anything done. Otherwise, the arrogance of the
mocker will continually lead him to take over the group and lead
it to unproductive and impossible ways.

The fool needs to be dealt with decisively, too. In his case,
he is to be struck with the rod and then avoided.

"A whip for the horse, a bridle for the donkey
    and a rod for the back of fools," 26:3.

Instead of driving her out of the community, however, the
wise will simply leave her presence.

"Leave the presence of a fool,
    for there you do not find words of knowledge," 14:7.

You leave the fool's presence because you realize that:

146

"Whoever walks with the wise becomes wise,
but the companion of fools suffers harm," 13:20.

You become like those with whom you associate or, alternatively said, you suffer the fate/enjoy the future of those you accompany. Fools may be frenzied, lack self-control, make bad decisions, lose their temper quickly and otherwise live ineffective lives, but they don't, in the eyes of Proverbs, carry with them the violence and danger of the mocker. Thus, it is best just not to associate with fools, even though at times you may have to speak to them so that they are not "wise in their own eyes," 26:5.

CONCLUSION—SOMETIMES YOU HAVE TO RUN

But when all is said about the matter, sometimes it isn't good for a wise person just quietly to leave the presence of a fool. At times, you have to run.

"The name of the Lord is a strong tower;
the righteous run into it and are safe," 18:10.

When evildoers assail, when the demands of foolish people become too great, when the chances are good that your own life of wisdom and attentiveness to your path becomes impossible, you need to run. The Psalmist captures the sentiment precisely:

"From the end of the earth I call to you, when my
heart is faint.
Lead me to the rock
that is higher than I;

For you are my refuge,
    a strong *tower* against the enemy," 61:2-3.

The one who runs isn't necessarily a cowardly person; s/ he just knows the things that are to be feared and avoided. But more than fearing and avoiding the fool, the wise person, or the person who aspires to wisdom, needs to follow a path—the path of wisdom. The next section of the book explores some major features of this path.

The Path of Wisdom

Day Fourteen

WISDOM'S WAY

IN CONTRAST TO THE FOOL and his folly is the wise and her wisdom. For Proverbs, wisdom is something that can be learned and applied to one's life. By applying it, one masters life. "For the wise the path of life leads upward," 15:24. Sorrow and loss no doubt enter into the life of the wise as well as the fool; but because the wise has submitted to a long course of instruction and discipline, she is able to master even the emergencies of life. The purpose of this and the next ten essays is to describe aspects of the life of wisdom. I have already made the case for wisdom's being the most important and most powerful thing in the world. In these essays I will analyze some aspects of the wise person's life, words and conduct that give her the unique ability to master the exigencies of life.

It all begins with thinking and speaking about the "way of wisdom." In fact, there is no concept more central to Proverbs than the way of wisdom. There are at least three Hebrew words which describe the way (we usually translate them as "way" or "path" or "steps"); the words occur in more than 100 places in Proverbs. Between 10-30% of Biblical uses of these terms are in Proverbs.

The "way of wisdom" anchors Proverbs' philosophy of life. Unlike most books of the Bible, Proverbs has the ambition of providing a fairly full philosophy of the good or blessed life. Most Biblical books address one particular issue or describe a period of Israelite history. Not Proverbs. Proverbs describes, like no other Biblical book with the possible exception of Leviticus, the full-orbed nature of the good life. Interestingly enough, in describing this life, the vocabulary of Proverbs is quite different from the "salvation-historical" terminology of Genesis or Exodus, or the "holiness/purity" terminology of Leviticus. We meet the language of wisdom in Proverbs.

So, how does one live wisely? This essay will seek to answer that question by looking at the way of wisdom from four perspectives. First, I will examine the *general contours* of the way of wisdom; then I will look at the way of wisdom as a path of *understanding or learning*. Third, I will pursue the way of wisdom as one of *critical thinking*. Fourth, I will finish the essay with an observation about *God's connection or relationship* to the way of wisdom.

THE GENERAL CONTOURS OF WISDOM

Most references to the way of wisdom occur in the first nine chapters of Proverbs. Let's begin with one of the clearest. The teacher says:

"I have taught you the way of wisdom;
I have led you in the paths of uprightness.

When you walk, your step will not be hampered;
   And if you run, you will not stumble.
Keep hold of instruction; do not let go;
   Guard her, for she is your life," 4:11-13.

Proverbs believes it is important for us to have a clear and unhampered way to go in life because so many things threaten to trip us up. We are distracted by alluring colors and sounds; we are kept from the right path by our desires and by boredom; we flag in zeal and suffer loss of heart. Our goal is to find a "level" way:

"the way of the lazy is overgrown with thorns,
   but the path of the upright is a level highway," 15:19.

Even though the path of the upright may smooth, level and clear of obstacles, there are many voices that try to lure us from it. What do those on the "other" paths say to us?

"Come with us, let us lie in wait for blood;
   let us wantonly ambush the innocent...
We shall find all kinds of costly things;
   We shall fill our house with booty," 1:11-13.

But the advice to keep to the path of wisdom is no less clear:

"my child, do not walk in their way,
   keep your foot from their paths;
for their feet run to evil,
   and they hurry to shed blood," 1:15-16.

151

Or, to put it positively,

> "Let your eyes look directly forward,
>   and your gaze be straight before you.
> Keep straight the path of your feet,
>   and all your ways will be sure.
> Do not swerve to the right or to the left;
>   Turn your foot away from evil," 4:25-27.

Someone may respond, "Well, the way of wisdom sounds more like the way of limited aspirations and ambition than a challenging and alluring life. I want to roam, explore, pursue my freedom, discover. How can the way of wisdom say anything to me?"

I think this is a wonderful question, and one that gets to the heart of what is meant by the "way of wisdom." Proverbs assumes that life consists of distractions and dangerous allurements as well as great and rewarding possibilities. It also knows that there are different kinds of people. People begin as rather naïve or gullible (*peti*). It never says how long the period or stage of gullibility lasts, but if it is not resolved into wisdom, the *peti* becomes a fool. A fool, as we have seen, is not a free person. She is controlled by emotions and by anger. Thus, the crucial choice in life for Proverbs is to adopt wisdom's way instead of the way of folly.

One of the chief differences between wisdom and folly is that the latter "looks to the ends of the earth," while the former "looks to wisdom," 17:24. Someone who looks to the ends of the earth is constantly distracted and can't quite get around to doing all that he knows he must do. He can't do this because he hasn't adopted a life of discipline and learning. You adopt that life by focusing your life. And you focus your life by stepping onto and keeping on the way of wisdom. That is the way that Proverbs conceptualizes it. The way of wisdom is a choice, but once you have made that choice, you are truly free. You are only free, however, if you recognize the fact that you must stay on the path, that you must continually commit yourself to the way of wisdom.

WISDOM AND LEARNING/UNDERSTANDING

"It is the wisdom of the clever to understand where
     they go,
   but the folly of fools misleads," 14:8.

Waltke translates the first, crucial, phrase a bit differently:

"The wisdom of the shrewd is to have insight into
     his way,
   but the folly of fools is deceit."

These two translations help us focus on one of the essential tasks or preoccupations of the person on the "way" of wisdom. It is to learn and then to assimilate what one learns. But here the language is very personal. The wise understand "where they go" or "have insight" into his/their way. The learning you collect by virtue of treading the way of wisdom isn't abstract; it isn't just learning for "learning's sake." It consists of gaining understanding or insight and bringing it into the flow of your life. I am convinced that all learning, for the wise person, can be integrated into his/her way, but the way of wisdom is to see how the insight you are developing and the knowledge you are gathering is knowledge of your way. Thus, one can look at the way of wisdom as a highway of sorts, down which many people who are wise go. But within that highway is a specially grooved path that is only yours, which only describes and characterizes your own life. The task of the wise is not simply to learn or to gather knowledge. It is to translate this knowledge into insight, into mastery so that it illumines and inspires you on the way.

You have insight into your way when you begin to understand your life theologically. That is, when you begin to see your life as shaped and led by God, you truly have insight into your way. But even as we gain insight into our way, we know that we don't fully *understand* our lives or our ways. Why? Because ultimately, as Proverbs teaches us:

> "All our steps are ordered by the Lord;
> how then can we understand our own ways?" 20:24.

In this regard, I believe that you never can have *too much* knowledge as you try to be true to your life in the way of wisdom. "An intelligent mind acquires knowledge, and the ear of the wise seeks knowledge," 18:15. Part of the joy of gaining insight into our way is to connect our diverse pieces of knowledge into a beautiful mosaic so that we have a deep sense that we are living a life of fruitfulness and helpfulness towards others.

THE WAY OF WISDOM AND CRITICAL THINKING

One of the criticisms usually leveled against people of faith is that the life of faith is either incompatible with or tends to denigrate critical thinking. I think the claim is completely fatuous, and Proverbs will help us show this to be the case. Before we get there, however, I agree that at one time it *may have been the case* that religious faith in general *discouraged* critical thinking. By that I mean that religious faith may have discouraged religious people from embracing worlds of science or other worlds that weren't based on Biblical authority. In some quarters that attitude still prevails. I think the proper way to express the correlation between lack of critical thinking and faith is as follows: wherever rigid orthodoxy prevails, critical thinking is endangered. By "rigid orthodoxy," I mean an approach to a subject that eliminates debate and tries to enforce uniform thinking. With this definition in mind, we may well discover that rigid orthodoxy prevails today more in non-religious than in religious areas.

As we turn to Proverbs, we see an emphasis not simply on gathering and assimilating knowledge but on judging things carefully.

"The simple believe everything,
    but the clever consider their steps," 14:15.

"The wicked put on a bold face,
    but the upright give thought to their ways," 21:29.

The first passage places the contrast between the simple and the wise/clever in how they look at information that comes their way. The simple just accredit or give credence to everything, while the wise keep a wary eye on their path. To keep a wary eye means that they discern, they weigh, they judge, they assess carefully whether the step they take is truly on the way or is misguided. Because the wise take so much care to cultivate and walk on the way, they have to consider, weigh and assess all information and knowledge that comes their way.

The second verse talks about two kinds of "faces" in life. The wicked put on a face of effrontery and confrontation, while the upright put on a "face" of discernment. Thought, rather than reckless action, characterizes the life of the wise.

The wise spends a good deal of his or her time in reflection on the path of wisdom. Such a style of living means that the wise person will bring an air of critical thought and analysis to everything he or she meets.

CONCLUSION—GOD AND THE WAY OF WISDOM

One can get the impression that following the way of wisdom is simply a mechanical exercise, and that once the right "input" is added, the right "output" (a blessed life) results. But Proverbs is too wise for that. It knows, for example:

> "The horse is made ready for the day of battle;
> but the victory belongs to the Lord," 21:31.

In language more appropriate to "way of wisdom" language, we find:

> "The human mind plans the way,
> but the Lord directs the steps," 16:9,

or,

> "The lot is cast into the lap,
> but the decision is the Lord's alone," 16:33.

We don't assure our way by walking in the way of wisdom. God alone assures it. But Proverbs is convinced that if we commit ourselves to this way, our life will be blessed indeed. Let's turn, in the next chapter, to the conduct and speech of the person who is walking in the path of wisdom.

Day Fifteen

PROVERBS 16:3; GETTING OUR BEARINGS ON WISDOM

"Commit your work to the Lord,
   and your plans will be established," 16:3

THOUGH SOMETIMES THE WISE sayings in Proverbs 10-29 appear in "mini-collections" of similar ideas (e.g., on the "fool" in 26:1-12; on the sovereignty of God in 16), most of them need to be savored in their rich individuality. But we can go further. Each individual proverb needs to be taken apart colon by colon and then word by word in order to enjoy the multi-faceted splendor of thought presented. You can't "speed read" Proverbs; they only reward those who read them slowly. To turn the verse from Habakkuk on its head, where the prophet was told to write the message large so that "he who runs may read" (Hab. 2:2), we could say that the unspoken message of the Book of Proverbs is that "only those who walk slowly may read."

Proverbs 16:3 is one such verse which repays slow reading, for once we pause over it we see that it expresses an idea which is precisely the opposite of what we would expect. We normally think of committing our *plans* to the Lord, and then watching to see how God's self-manifestation happens in our subsequent *work*. In other words, we usually think that dreams come before instantiation and fulfillment of dreams. Indeed, the popular culture around us tells us to "dream big" or to "envision the future" as a way of helping to influence or even effect that future or that dream. Life coaches and others often tell us to "imagine ourselves doing" what we would think of as a successful outcome.

This attitude prevails everywhere. When I was interviewed for a legal job several years ago, the first question the interviewer asked me was, "Where do you want to be in three to five years?" That is, in the language of Proverbs 16:3, 'what are your plans'? Or, again, when a person who wanted me to invest in his company told me why I should do so, he said, "By the end of 2010 (18 months from the time of this writing), this should be a multi-million dollar business." We have to "sell" plans, a future, in order to get people to act today. That is the way that most of us live our lives. It seems true, then, that the person of faith would want to commit *plans* to God as the first priority in living the wise life. Commit plans to God and then work will be established. That is the way we tend to think.

THE FLOW OF PROVERBS 16:3

We think this way. Until we take some time with Proverbs 16:3. The verse says the opposite. Let's first consider the flow of the Hebrew, then reflect on what it suggests about life and then

160

illustrate its truth by reference to an important philosopher in the West. My point will be that the received wisdom of our culture, in being concerned about *future* plans, is trumped by the biblical emphasis or focus on fidelity and engagement *today*.

The Hebrew verse consists of only six words. The verb translated "commit" is the Hebrew word for "roll" or "unfold." When it is read with the following word for "to" or "unto" (*el*), we have a phrase that is pronounced "*gol-el.*" It "rolls" on the tongue—just as the word literally is translated. Thus, we unroll, unfurl, or roll onto God our *maaseka*—our "works" or our "deeds." The verb behind *maaseka* is the simple Hebrew word for "do" or "make." Since the imperative is in the present tense, the first colon is well rendered, "continually roll along to God your works." Thus, we focus on the present works of our hands. What are you doing today? Right now. NO! Don't write on your Facebook Wall to tell me about it, roll it along to God. That is the thought of Proverbs.

What is the result? The last two words tell us: our plans will be established. The Hebrew word for "plans" is derived from the verb *hashab*, which means to "intend" or to "plan" something. The passive voice of the verb translated "establish", in the future tense, expresses the certainty of these plans coming to pass. In contrast to the first colon, the second colon talks about the future, and talks about generic plans, rather than specific works.

THINKING ABOUT THE PROVERB

The brilliance of the proverb rests in its ease of application and its encouragement to think of what is directly before you. It can easily be applied because we always know what our "works" are at the present moment. Sometimes it is hard to perceive our plans or intentions. They change; they are fuzzy. But not so our works. Even if we are simply daydreaming, we are aware of what we are doing. Daydreaming. So, commit that to God. Roll it along to God. "God, take even my daydreams and use them for your glory." "God, I don't know how this seeming distraction in my day works towards my grand plans, but I unfurl it to you in faith." By encouraging us to think of what is directly before us, this proverb is consistent with the entire message of Proverbs— the wise person attends to his/her way, to the tasks at hand, to the contours of his or her steps (cf. 14:15). It is the fool whose eyes are directed to "the ends of the earth" (17:24). Wisdom is fundamentally discovered by taking care of the tasks before us. Each day. As Proverbs 16:20 says:

"Those who are attentive to a matter will prosper,
and happy are those who trust in the Lord."

Thus, the philosophy of Proverbs is one of wholehearted engagement with our present tasks. Wisdom is to be found in attentiveness to the tasks of the day, and in rolling those along to God. If one does that faithfully, one's plans for the future will be established. Our concern, however, is for the present and not for the future. Our eyes are directed back to the affairs right before our eyes, rather than to the gossamer hopes and uncertain longings of our hearts.

A WORD FROM A PHILOSOPHER

This idea of the blessedness of the present, of present activities fraught with meaning, is strikingly confirmed in the work of the French romantic philosopher Jean-Jacques Rousseau

(1712-1778). In the passage to be quoted, he is talking about happiness, that most elusive of virtues. His philosophy in general shares little in common with Proverbs. Indeed, Rousseau's 1762 education classic *Emile or On Education* lays out the philosophy of child-centered self-discovery, which is quite absent from Proverbs. See, however, my treatment of a special proverb on education, 22:6, in Day 27. Yet, Rousseau's commitment to defining happiness in terms of embracing the present is quite consistent with Proverbs. Philosopher Simon Critchley, writing in the *New York Times*, gives us this arresting passage from Rousseau's "Reveries of a Solitary Walker,"

> "If there is a state where the soul can find a
> resting-place secure enough to establish itself and
> concentrate its entire being there, with no need to
> remember the past or reach into the future, where
> time is nothing to it, where the present runs on
> indefinitely but this duration goes unnoticed, with
> no sign of the passing of time, and no other feeling
> of deprivation or enjoyment, pleasure or pain,
> desire or fear than the simple feeling of existence, a
> feeling that fills our soul entirely, as long as this state
> lasts, we can call ourselves happy, not with a poor,
> incomplete and relative happiness such as we find in
> the pleasures of life, but with a sufficient, complete
> and perfect happiness which leaves no emptiness to
> be filled in the soul."[1]

---

1   Quoted in J. Mason, *The Indispensable Rousseau* (1979), pp. 88-89. Critchley's column, entitled "Happy Like God," appeared in the *New York Times* online version of May 27, 2009.

If we take *that* present, the present which "runs on indefinitely but (whose) duration goes unnoticed, with no sign of the passing of time," a present so full because we realize that it contains our works, and if we roll that present along to God, we may just find that our plans become part of that ever-enjoyable and powerful present. We will discover how plans *become* works, and the plans to be established *become* the works that were committed to God. Thus, with Rousseau, let's stretch out that present almost interminably, unfurling it as we go to God, and then the plans will fade imperceptibly into the works, which works are continually committed back in praise to God.

Day Sixteen

WISDOM'S ETHICS I—MANAGING THE HEART

INTRODUCTION

WHEN I WAS a college student in the early 1970s, while the United States was still mired in the Viet Nam war, ethics was all the rage. What was a just war? What were our moral obligations towards the poor? How do we respond morally to a world of scarcity? Then, as the 1970s wore on, ethics, if possible, became *even more* the rage. As a result of the fall-out from the Watergate scandal, ethics courses became mandatory at most professional schools--from business, to law to medicine. Thus, to have been a trained ethicist at the end of the 1970s was like being a psychologist in the 1980s, an economist in the 1990s and a security consultant in the 2000s. Everyone wanted you.

An unexamined assumption of those days with respect to ethics, which continues in our day, was that the contours of ethics as a field were quite easily defined. After all, if you call on an ethicist or think you need an ethicist, you should only expect to pay big bucks for someone who knows what ethics is. My contention in this and the next essay is that the field of ethics as it was then taught (and is currently taught) ignores crucial issues about what constitutes the right way to live and that the Book of Proverbs provides strikingly useful and powerful advice in the area of what is lacking.

In a word, the traditional approach to ethics *assumes* and *assumed* that the principal issues that *everyone* wants to solve are social issues.[1] These problems may also in some sense be "personal" issues, such as one's attitude towards abortion or gay rights, but ethics as taught by the practitioners focuses on what I will call "ethics as issues." Issues are problems that need to be identified, studied, and solved. Ethics helps you do that within the framework of being a morally good person.

The problem with this kind of focus on ethics, I discovered in the 1970s, was that even with the focus on "ethics as issues," the whole field just seemed too abstract to me. World hunger or scarcity was hardly a burning issue as I saw my fraternity brothers wolfing down helpings of food. Thus, in order to help simulate what privation was, or what difficult choices meant, professors put us, figuratively speaking, "in a lifeboat." "Lifeboat ethics" was the approach to ethics that assumed you had scarce resources and too many people to consume the resources.[2] It was as if you had 20 people in a lifeboat that would hold 12 safely. How do you decide, for the sake of saving 12, to get rid of the other eight?

Well, I pondered this sort of problem with my other co-confused 19 year-old colleagues, and I concluded in the end that

1   A good summary of five leading ethical theories in our day is here: http://www.scu.edu/ethics/practicing/decision/thinking.html.

2   A primer on lifeboat ethics is here: http://en.wikipedia.org/wiki/Lifeboat_ethics.

I didn't know which eight people I would get rid of, but I was secretly hoping that the professor would be one of the eight! That is, I became frustrated because I felt that ethics was so far removed from actual reality to be a useless undertaking. I adopted that approach to ethics until I discovered what I consider to be the ethics of Proverbs. In a word, ethics for Proverbs has more to do with "personal management" than "ethics as issues."

THE ETHICS OF THE BOOK OF PROVERBS

If you wanted to find what professional ethicists call "ethical principles" in Proverbs, they are easy to spot. We are told time and again that unjust balances are an abomination to the Lord (20:10, 23). We know that showing partiality is not a good thing (28:21). We are told to live with integrity (19:1). Proverbs especially shows a concern for the welfare of the poor, grounding our concern for the poor in God's love (17:5). Other examples can easily be multiplied.

Yet it is striking to me how little emphasis is placed on these supposedly important principles in a book that takes care to spell out the blessed or good life. Does Proverbs really not understand ethics? Or, might it be so "eternally" minded that this world is unimportant? To the latter question one rejoins, quickly, "No!" Proverbs doesn't even contemplate a future condition after death. Instead, the most important issues to Proverbs are how you control yourself and how you speak. "Personal management," rather than "ethics as issues," is the focus of Proverbs' concern. Ethics, for Proverbs, is grounded on your becoming a better person, and your becoming a better person is rooted primarily in your self-control and your skillful use of words.

When I realized that ethics could be so defined and that,

in fact, Proverbs so defined it, I became fired with enthusiasm. Finally, I thought, *here* is an ethics that won't bore me, because here is instruction about how, actually, to become a better person. It is futile to solve the world's problems if you haven't, in the meantime, learned how to control your rage and to express yourself skillfully.

A PRIMER ON PROVERBS' ETHICS

Ethics in Proverbs is connected with two kinds of control: that of the mind/heart/self and that of the lips. In this essay I will touch on four principles of "mind" or "heart" control. The next essay will consider our use of words.

Let's begin, even before reaching the first of our four principles, with a statement of Proverbs' approach to self-control.

> "One who is slow to anger is better than the mighty,
>   and one whose temper is controlled than one
>   who captures a city," 16:32.

> "Like a city breached, without walls,
>   is one who lacks self-control," 25:28.

Make no mistake about it. Military victories are important and, in a culture like Israel where you are generally despised by your neighbors, are very important. But Proverbs is bold enough to say that the one who manages the temper is better than the general who captures the city. Now we are *really* taking ethics. *Now* we are getting personal about it. Isn't that, in fact, the root meaning of *ethos*—"character"?[3] Well, how does this self-control work?

1. Learning How To Listen

First, you control your heart/mind by learning how to listen.

"If one gives answer before hearing,
it is folly and shame," 18:13.

Learning how to listen can be one of life's most rewarding lessons. The fool, we have learned, takes no pleasure in listening, but only in expressing personal opinion (18:2). Thus, the fool is one who interrupts, discounts or ignores what another says, and is so hell bent on his personal agenda that he makes himself objectionable to people. But this proverb tells us only to answer after giving a hearing to someone. Is this something that just "comes naturally" or do we need to learn techniques, skills, etc. to be able to listen? In my experience it is a matter of technique. Two important sub-skills to master in order to listen well are to remove your emotions from the encounter and learn how to ask basic questions of a speaker that will aid him/her in telling the story. Establishing an emotional "coolness" or "distance" from the concerns of a speaker, even if you happen to have a personal stake in the issue, is a technique that can be learned by practice. Then, you learn to "flesh out" a person's story, a story that is sometimes breathlessly told, by interjecting simple, crucial and clarifying questions in the narrative.

---

3   The *Oxford English Dictionary*, under "ethic," reminds us that its root meaning, from the Greek, is "character."

2. Developing a "Cool" Temperament

Second, as just hinted at, you control your heart/mind by developing a "cool" temperament. Much of the wisdom literature in the ancient Near East reflected on two types of temperament — the "warm" and the "cool," and taught its adherents to practice the latter. Proverbs fits into this tradition — warning us against the "hothead" in 22:24 or 29:22. Proverbs has this to say:

"One who spares words is knowledgeable;
   one who is cool in spirit has understanding," 17:27.

"A tranquil mind gives life to the flesh,
   but passion makes the bones rot," 14:30.

The Hebrew of the first colon of 14:30 is even more arresting: literally it reads, "the life of the body, a calm heart."[4] That is, the tranquil mind or cool mind or calm heart is actually the life, the source of vitality of the body for the wise person. It isn't just something that you might try to aspire to every once in a while. It is vital for life.

We have seen how this kind of heart or mind is contrasted with that of the fool, who is quick to anger, who is angry "on the same day" (12:15) as his provocation. The urgent ethical question, then, is not how we might stop war in the next generation but how we attain a tranquil mind. Do we do so by engagement, retreat, speaking little, self-discipline, listening to our IPODS as we walk down the pathway? Since one of the purposes of Biblical study is to get a good discussion going, I think we have just identified a question on that issue.

---

4   So translated in Roland Murphy, *Proverbs* (Word, 1998), p. 101.

3. Learning How To Ponder

Third, we develop self-control by learning how to think and ponder issues. The wise may often have an "answer" to a problem immediately upon considering it, but the crucial issue here is to answer with apt words at the appropriate time. Note the contrast in the verbs between the two types of people:

"The mind of the righteous ponders how to answer,
but the mouth of the wicked pours out evil," 15:28.

The Hebrew verb "ponder" (*hagah* literally means to murmur or meditate) is used about 20 times in the Bible, but its most significant parallel usages are when the issue of meditating, cogitating and reflection are in view. Three such usages are:

"My soul is feasted as with a rich feast,
and my mouth praises you with joyful lips
when I think of you on my bed,
and meditate (*hagah*) on you in the watches of
the night," Ps. 63:5-6.

"I will call to mind the deeds of the Lord;
I will remember your wonders of old.
I will meditate (*hagah*) on all your work,
And muse on your mighty deeds," Ps. 77:11-12.

"Happy are those
who do not follow the advice of the wicked,
or take the path that sinners tread,
or sit in the seat of scoffers;
but their delight is in the law of the Lord,

and on his law they meditate (*hagah*) day and
night," Ps. 1:1-2.

The verb "ponder" in 15:28 is important because it suggests
not simply a technique to master but a style of living—where
one, as it were, retreats into one's inscrutability to consider the
aspects of an issue, only to appear and declare one's piece, before
retreating back to that sacred place of pondering.[5] By pondering
over an issue, one breaks the cycle of foolishness endemic in
our world—the cycle that leads from utterance to comment to
umbrage being taken to more utterance to more comment.

4. Taking An Insult

Fourth, the person exercising self-control knows how to
take an insult. Or, to put it differently, wisdom ethics teaches
us that bearing others' foolishness, ill-tempered rants, imprecise
observations and scathing attacks is an essential aspect of learning
wisdom.

"Fools show their anger at once,
but the prudent ignore an insult," 12:16.

"Those with good sense are slow to anger,
and it is their glory to overlook an offense," 19:11.

This is one of the hardest lessons for one who wants to
practice self-control, because it is not only tempting but sometimes
seemingly *obligatory* to respond to a fool's provocation. Indeed,

---

5   I owe the notion of the "inscrutability" of the wise person to scattered
references in Bruce's Waltke's two-volume commentary, *The Book of Proverbs*
(2004-05).

if you don't stand up for yourself, who will? If you don't correct a fool, she may become wise in her own eyes (26:5). But maturation comes when you bear the stripes of abuse hurled in your direction.

I have learned that one of the tactics of a mocker or a fool is to try to get you "off your game" by saying inappropriate things or baiting you into responding with anger. The ways they do this are legion—from criticizing your work obliquely or directly, to praising their own efforts, to misrepresenting the nature of communications, to using loaded rhetoric that is calculated to throw things into confusion. But if you truly want to address a larger issue, and not become side-tracked by personal invective, you have to be the one to ignore the insult or overlook the offense. Indeed, if you learn to do this, you confirm in your experience that the one who controls his spirit is better than one capturing a city.

CONCLUSION

Once you begin to see the primary ethical dimension in Proverbs as learning how to control the self, rather than how to allocate scarce resources or solve the problems of poverty or war, the book opens to you like a magic door. You push gently and it springs open, firing you with enthusiasm to become a modern-day sage. But we aren't yet finished with the ethics of Proverbs. It also includes how we speak. Let's now turn to that subject.

Day Seventeen

WISDOM'S ETHICS II—THE WAY YOU SAY THINGS

THE PREVIOUS CHAPTER may have left you with the impression that the wise person is a sort of hermit or, at least, one who very reluctantly engages with the world. Not so. The wise person is just starkly aware of how much debility, distraction and unnecessary waste there is in unfruitful engagement with people. Unfruitful connection with people is doubly harmful; first, it doesn't yield a productive time with the other and, second, it takes the wise person away from her own cultivation of wisdom. Fools, who greatly outnumber the wise, waste your time and don't use words properly or well. In the language of Ecclesiastes:

> "Words spoken by the wise bring them favor,
>   but the lips of fools consume them.
> The words of their mouths begin in foolishness,

And their talk ends in wicked madness;
Yet fools talk on and on," 10:12-14.

The wise person in Proverbs is particularly attentive
to the words she uses. Four aspects of good words should be
mentioned: their content, their form, the manner in which they
are said, and their timeliness. Mastery of words in all of these
contexts is crucial for effective and wise communication. The
Book of Proverbs places particular attention on the form and
timeliness of words. It is a large part of the wisdom's ethics to
know *how* to say something well and *when* to say it. This chapter
will probe Proverbs' understanding of words by looking at five
topics: words as a "life or death" matter; words that "fit"; soft
and gentle words; words and learning; and the results of good
words.

1. Words—A Life or Death Matter

Most people treat words as if they were bricks. For them,
words are relatively undifferentiated, cheap and useful for
erecting almost any verbal structure you want. Proverbs is much
more sophisticated than that. It realizes that words are a matter
of life and death.

"Death and life are in the power of the tongue,
and those who love it will eat its fruits," 18:21.

This unusually-phrased proverb gives us pause. The
tongue, the user of words, has death and life in its grip. Each can
flow from it. The tongue can wound or kill; it can stifle creativity;
it can take away every measure of joy that a person tries to
celebrate. Or, it can bring life. Its tenor, timing and content can

inspire, encourage, open a heart, solidify a relationship, create beauty that the world has not yet seen. If we truly were aware of how lethal or life-giving the tongue is, we would hire a guard for it, to make sure it is only used properly.

The second colon of the verse suggests that those who love it (the power of the tongue) will eat its fruits (i.e., it will either bring life or death to them). Not everyone is either aware of or loves the power of the tongue. To them, after all, words are just bricks. The person who loves the tongue can be either wise or foolish; he has simply caught on to the tremendous power resident in this organ. Such a person will enjoy the fruits of the tongue, whether for life or death.

Another verse connecting the tongue with life and death is 13:3,

> "Those who guard their mouths preserve their lives,
>   those who open wide their lips come to ruin."

A quotation from an Old Testament apocryphal book says it well (Sir. 28:25):

> "Make balances and scales for your words,
>   and make a door and a bolt for your mouth,"

The wise person guards her most precious things. She "weighs" her words. Care for words gives you your life.

2. Words That Fit

A word "fits" when it has all the right features: content, form, expressiveness, timeliness. A great irony, perhaps intended by the author of Proverbs but lost on us today because we don't generally know Hebrew, is that the most familiar verse describing the "fitness" of speech is untranslatable. Well, many translations have it as follows:

> "A word fitly spoken
> is like apples of gold in a setting of silver," 25:11.

Yet Murphy and Waltke, two of the more helpful commentators on the language of Proverbs, both point out that there are at least three translation difficulties in the verse. First, we don't know exactly how to translate "setting." Even the Greek translation of the Bible, made within a few hundred years of Proverbs, rendered it fairly wildly--"on a necklace of carnelian."[1] The second difficulty is in a proper rendering of the euphonic phrase *dabar dabur* ("word spoken"). Waltke isn't satisfied with the traditional translation of these two words, and decides to render it "a decision made."[2] I will stay with the traditional translation, because it is consistent with the general flow of Proverbs. Finally, no one quite knows what the phrase "fitly spoken" really means. Waltke calls it an "obscure *hapax legomenon*" (word or phrase appearing one time in the Bible).[3]

My case for "fitness" in speaking doesn't rest fully on 25:11, but I bring it up because Proverbs may be speaking to us "tongue in cheek" at this point. Until 25:11 Proverbs has emphasized strongly the importance of proper speech. Speech, as we just saw, is a life or death matter. Yet, when we think about this too often we begin to get *real serious* about speech, as if weighing each word is like weighing gold. But this kind of living is too self-conscious for the author of Proverbs and for anyone who wants

---

1   Quoted in Roland Murphy, *Proverbs*, p. 189, note 11a.

2   Bruce Waltke, *The Book of Proverbs, 15-31*, p. 320.

3   *Ibid.*

to live freely and from the heart. So, Proverbs subtly undermines itself by re-emphasizing the importance of fitting words—in a sentence that uses words that don't really "fit." We should smile, realize our humanity and weakness, commit ourselves again to good words but recognize that a few "word surds" will slip in now and again.

A "better" verse to make the point is from 15:23,

> "To make an apt answer is a joy to anyone,
>   and a word in season, how good it is!"

The literal rendering of the verse might give it more sheen:

> "Joy for a person is in the answer of the mouth,
>   and a word in its time—how good!"

The verse especially emphasizes the seasonableness of a word. When a good word comes at the right time, it is as if the universe "clicks" into place, and the natural reaction we have is "how good!" It just "fits." Spend your life searching for and uttering those types of words and you will have spent your life well.

3. Soft And Gentle Words

We hear it all the time—"I don't object to *what* you say; it is *the way* you say it that bothers me." People are often unaware of how they "come across." Their tone and language can be hostile, aggressive, aloof, menacing and still they might not notice it. The key to a wise use of words, for Proverbs, is to cultivate softness and gentleness in speech. "Real men" speak gently. Let's look at four crucial verses on this subject:

"A soft answer turns away wrath,
    but a harsh word stirs up anger," 15:1.

"A gentle tongue is a tree of life,
    but perverseness in it breaks the spirit," 15:4.

"Pleasant words are like a honeycomb,
    Sweetness to the soul and health to the body," 16:24.

"With patience a ruler may be persuaded,
    and a soft tongue can break bones," 25:15.

Reading and re-reading these verses gives one the impression that the wise person is a kind of "word surgeon." Incisions are made carefully; bones are handled gently; tissue is caressed softly. Each of these verses invites detailed consideration, but a few points will have to suffice. The first verse appears in the context of its preceding verse, 14:35, regarding the wrath of kings. A wise person can even deflect the king's wrath, but must do it with "soft" words. The word "soft" is translated "tender" elsewhere (4:3) and suggests words that are delicate, soft, tender and gentle. Waltke notes that its appearance with the word "answer" suggests "a response that both in substance and style soothes and comforts the listener."[4]

Introduction of the phrase "tree of life" in 15:4 evokes in the reader/reciter a sense that gentle words can even restore paradise. Indeed, that is what it sounds like when a gentle and appropriate word is spoken. It is as if an unworldly or hitherto

---

4   *Book of Proverbs, 1-15*, p. 613.

inaccessible peace is gained. Finally, the last proverb is arresting because of its surprising conclusion. The tongue, a soft organ, is properly used when it utters gentle words. But the result of gentle words is fractured bones. Here the meaning is *not*, of course, that soft words bring discord and pain, but that gentle words, spoken over a long period of time, can wear down and even obliterate the toughest opposition. If we really believed this to be the case, each of us would enroll in "wisdom 101," which unfortunately isn't taught at any college, as far as I know.

4. Words And Learning

Though much has been said about the form and timeliness of words, their inextricable connection with knowledge and its diffusion needs emphasis. One uses words not just to avert anger or to heal the soul; they are also the chief means of communicating knowledge. The Hebrew text of 15:2 helps us immensely.

Its traditional translation is bland:

"The tongue of the wise dispenses knowledge,
    but the mouths of fools pour out folly," 15:2.

A more literal translation of the first colon yields: "the tongue of the wise makes knowledge good." Or, massaging it only a little, "the tongue of the wise adorns knowledge" or "makes knowledge attractive." I think the last translation has significant allure. What might it mean that the tongue of the wise makes knowledge attractive?

Let's think about learning today. Some would say that we are always learning, and there is some truth to that. But learning is also a formal process, one which is engaged in each day by millions and millions in the USA and hundreds of millions worldwide. My experience as a teacher for 25 years is that learning is painful for most students. The primary motivation for learning is a test that looms, a degree that beckons and a career that pays well. Learning has to be endured so that the prize can be gained. Therefore, for the rest of life, adults believe that formalized learning is something that kids do, or that kids and young people must do, and not something that adults should engage in. Most of this flows from the fact that learning never was made attractive to the adults when they were children.

The wise person is defined as one who knows how to make learning attractive to people. She has assessed the temperament and learning styles of the student, she has mastered the content of what she wants to communicate, she knows how to swathe things in beautiful language, she speaks things in a timely and apt fashion. Studies have been done on almost everything that contributes to inefficiency or productivity loss in business, but I think that two ignored areas are the way that learning is done and how well interpersonal and official communication takes place. The wise person makes learning a beautiful experience. He brings the learner right into the awesome presence of the thing to be learned, whether it is an oak or a symphony, and he unfolds the essence of that thing to the learner. If a word in season (15:23) is greeted with an immediate "how good!", then "making knowledge beautiful" ought to be greeted with the same eagerness. When knowledge is made beautiful, our world will flourish.

Several other verses talk about learning and wisdom. One more will have to suffice. In 15:7, the wise person is said to scatter knowledge:

"The lips of the wise spread knowledge,
    not so the minds of fools."

This verse is surprising at first glance, especially given the words of the previous essay, but it represents one side of a very healthy paradox. The wise person does spread knowledge; the verb suggests a kind of flinging of it far and wide. Let the world know that knowledge is here, and that the wise strives to make it beautiful.

CONCLUSION—THE RESULTS OF GOOD SPEECH

Fruitful metaphors tumble from the pages of Proverbs when the end of good speech is envisioned.

"The mouth of the righteous is a fountain of life,
    but the mouth of the wicked conceals violence," 10:11.

"Rash words are like sword thrusts,
    but the tongue of the wise brings healing," 12:18.

"Anxiety weighs down the heart,
    but a good word cheers it up," 12:25.

And, finally, in a proverb that all lovers ought to embrace,

"One who gives an honest answer
    gives a kiss on the lips," 24:26.

Such is the ethics of wisdom. It begins with self-control, it leads through proper speech and it ends with a kiss on the lips. Who wouldn't want this kind of wisdom?

183

Day Eighteen

PROVERBS 20:22; BREAKING THE CYCLE OF FOOLISHNESS

"Do not say, 'I will repay evil.' Wait for the Lord,
   and he will help you," 20:22.

ON FIRST EXAMINATION, we see that this verse teaches a lesson that is repeated throughout the Scriptures. "'Vengeance is mine, I will repay,' says the Lord," Rom. 12:19. Or, more elaborately and eloquently:

"Vengeance is mine, and recompense,
   for the time when their foot shall slip;
because the day of their calamity is at hand,
   their doom comes swiftly," Deut. 32:35.

Proverbs elsewhere expresses a similar thought:

"Do not say, 'I will do to others as they have done to me;
   I will pay them back for what they have done,'" 24:29.

We have heard it over and over. Don't retaliate. God will judge. Our task is to turn the other cheek. We hear verses like this so often that meaning is drained from the thought. It simply becomes a command like many other Biblical commands, and we do with it what we do with most other commands in our life. We ignore it. Or, more colorfully, we shuffle it along with other familiar verses like so many faded playing cards, and then play our tired old games with it. Or to change the metaphor, we have a collection of Scriptural thoughts that looks more like a defanged lion than a two-edged sword.

But when we look more closely at Proverbs 20:22, we see this word of advice in the context of the ways that wise and foolish people act, and it takes on a whole new universe of meaning. In short, this verse can best be understood in the context of the response of the wise person to provocation by fools. The wise person is to "wait" and not to respond. By learning how to wait for the Lord's action, the wise person has a good chance of breaking the cycle of foolishness which threatens to overwhelm us and everyone else in life. By not retaliating or responding to the fool, the wise person trusts that God will send help in God's good and mysterious time.

THINKING ABOUT BREAKING CYCLES

Whenever we pick up a newspaper or journal today, we are confronted with the phrase "breaking the cycle." A quick web search reveals that there exist groups that help you break the cycle of violence or poverty or domestic abuse or homelessness or drug addiction or hopelessness or eating disorders or a variety of other human ills. In fact, that phrase only entered into American speech in the late 1970s. A search of the most detailed legal data base I could find revealed that there was only one appearance of the phrase "breaking the cycle" before 1975, and that usage appeared in a the context of the operation of a machine—you break its cycle of operation.

Those who love language and the connection of ideas and words might pause to ask the question not only of what "breaking the cycle" means, but why it only was introduced in the last 30 or 35 years in our speech. It seemed to arise at the time of and in connection with our increased societal awareness of debilitating ills that disempower people. Indeed, the word disempower, in the way that most of us understand it today (rendering a group or individual powerless) was never used in the current sense before 1960. We invented an entire language of disability and ability in the 1960s and 1970s to correspond to our societal focus on mistreated or ignored groups in American life. My thesis is that groups in power, who wanted to share some of the power (or empower) with others, began using the language of "breaking the cycle" as a shorthand way of saying that they supported new opportunities for historically marginalized or oppressed groups. When those in power began to use the phrase, those who represented oppressed groups quickly glommed onto it, especially in making requests of foundations or governments for money. Their program, they claimed, would "break the cycle" of some social ill. Soon everyone began to use the phrase, but few gave much consideration to how much effort it actually takes to change the life circumstances of one person or one family. Those who glibly talked about "breaking the cycle" were probably aware that you just don't spring people out of poverty, violence, addiction and other ills; nevertheless, the language took over our modes of communication.

I recall hearing the phrase for the first time in the early 1980s just after I had moved to Oregon from Europe. A senior Oregon political figure was speaking about social ills that plagued us. What we needed to do, he intoned, was to help free people from their debilitating conditions. We needed to "break the cycle" of violence, poverty and hopelessness. I thought the phrase sounded so noble and powerful the first time I heard it. The politician also spoke that day of getting to the "root causes" and not simply the "symptoms" of something. He really had his rhetoric down...

MOVING TO PROVERBS

"Breaking the cycle," then, became a homespun phrase that sounded like it meant something—but really didn't. It became a way for people to sound like they really were doing something to effect change when they really weren't. Thus, the title of this chapter is a little tongue in cheek—a spoof on the concept of "breaking the cycle." But there is also a serious point to be made here—the way of non-retaliation is taught in Proverbs 20:22 not so much because of the value of forgiveness for the soul of the forgiver but because of the need of the wise to establish the superiority of the way of wisdom over the way of folly. Non-retaliation, for Proverbs, demonstrates the supremacy of the way of wisdom.

Here is the thought behind Prov. 20:22. The hallmark of the fool in Proverbs is that he speaks his mind before thinking, he doesn't listen to anyone else, he is easily angered and is unconcerned about the consequences of his action. The fool is, in short, a reactive person. Stimuli are presented; the fool reacts. It is as predictable as the rain in an Oregon winter. Some verses give the flavor of the fool.

188

"A fool takes no pleasure in understanding,
   but only in expressing personal opinion," 18:2.

"A rebuke strikes deeper into a discerning person
   than a hundred blows into a fool," 17:10.

"Fools show their anger at once,
   but the prudent ignore an insult," 12:16.

"The wise are cautious and turn away from evil,
   but the fool throws off restraint and is careless," 14:16.

Proverbs never tells us how many fools there are in the world, but the impression given is that this kind of foolish behavior characterizes much of human dealing. Thus, it wouldn't be a stretch to argue, and it is confirmed by our experience, that foolishness, when left unchecked, simply multiplies itself and begins to dominate the public square and human organizations in general. Foolishness is to the public square as English Ivy is to the garden. It takes over unless you are vigilant to prevent it.

The greatest temptation for the wise or the one who aspires to wisdom is to be caught up in the waves of foolishness that are breaking constantly on our shore. The temptation, in the words of Proverbs, is "to answer a fool according to his folly"—i.e., to respond to the fool. But that kind of response risks implicating the wise or aspiring wise person in the cycle of endless foolishness, recrimination, anger, thoughtlessness and, ultimately, death. So, in order for wisdom to have an effective voice in the public square, in the private company, in the family or in a life with friends, it must not get caught up in the WHOOSH of the fool.

Several proverbs mention this:

> "Whoever belittles another lacks sense,
>   but an intelligent person remains silent," 11:12.

> "Fools show their anger at once,
>   but the prudent ignore an insult," 12:16.

> "When words are many, transgression is not lacking,
>   but the prudent are restrained in speech," 10:19.

> "The mind of the righteous ponders how to answer,
>   but the mouth of the wicked pours out evil," 15:28.

> "Whoever is slow to anger has great understanding,
>   but one who has a hasty temper exalts folly," 14:29.

Additional examples can be multiplied. The hallmark of prudent or wise people is they consider the path before them. They do not react hastily. They, as it were, let the noise of the fool die down and fade away completely before responding. They don't get caught up in the show and desperation, in the rage and demand, in the arrogance and deception, in the desire only to express an opinion. They, instead, want wisdom to reign. They want instruction to be the foundational principle of life. So, they/we wait. And, as the passage promises, the result is not the judgment on the fool, though that is assumed, but the help that will come to those who wait. "Breaking the cycle" of foolishness through waiting, even when it looks tantalizingly attractive to respond to a fool's provocation, is the way of wisdom. There will be a time when help will come. You can bank on it.

Day Nineteen

KNOWLEDGE ACQUITISION AND WISDOM

"An intelligent mind acquires knowledge,
   and the ear of the wise seeks knowledge," Prov. 18:15.

"The mind of one who has understanding seeks
   knowledge,
   but the mouths of fools feed on folly," Prov. 15:14.

YESTERDAY I WAS WATCHING the National Spelling Bee, where kids 10 –14 years old demonstrate feats of spelling brilliance which few adults can match. Reactions from adults on seeing these performances range from, "How amazingly impressive!" to "This is just a sophisticated form of child abuse!" In fact, each year there are protestors at the Bee from the Simplified Spelling Society (SSS), who argue that the complexity of English, which the Bee celebrates, actually leads to problems like dyslexia and lack of interest in reading.

My approach is neither to criticize the bee nor exalt too

highly those who compete, but to say that spelling is important if it leads to a love of learning. Impressive as correct spelling is (and I have twice placed second in the National Senior Spelling Bee), the goal of spelling for me is to probe the world *behind* the words or the worlds into which words lead us. In that regard, I think that most adults watch the competition for a different reason. Most watch it to be impressed, amazed, or entertained. Instead of admiring accomplishment, amazing as it is, I watch the bees to get more words that I can study, write about, internalize, and use to expand my understanding of the worlds which the words open to me.

For example, one of the words in Round Three of the 2009 Bee was *ceremoniarius*. I probably could have spelled the word correctly, but I didn't know what it meant. So, I decided to spend 30 minutes with *ceremoniarius* to see what it would tell me about itself.[1] I learned that it had to do with an official who long ago superintended all things about a religious service, especially in a Catholic or Episcopal church. But this wasn't enough for me, and so I discovered, in my search, the names of the people a *ceremoniarius* might supervise/advise, from the "celebrant" to the "boat boy."[2] And then, as Robert Frost says, "way leads to way" and I ended up studying about "boat boys" and "thurifers" and many other things and persons I hadn't previously studied. I was gaining knowledge, knowledge that I could then file away in my mind, knowledge that might have seemed to lack utility in the moment but which I know will come in handy sometime in the future.

I tell this story because many people have the impression

---

1   The fuller results of my study on *ceremoniarius* are here: http://www.drbilllong.com/2008WordsV/2009BeeII.html

2   http://en.wikipedia.org/wiki/Boat_boy.

that knowledge isn't too helpful unless it is "useful," whatever that means. People have quoted the verse from Paul to me, "Knowledge puffs up but loves builds up" (I Cor. 8:1) as a sort of club to use against those who seek knowledge. At one time I was intimidated by those who quoted the verse; no longer. Now, I am an unabashed knowledge seeker. The point of this essay, and the verses I will exposit, is that knowledge is key to the life of wisdom, and the path of wisdom is studded with nuggets of knowledge.

RELATING TO KNOWLEDGE

The word "know" or "knowledge" appears hundreds of times in the Bible, and its meaning runs the gamut from the most intimate form of human connection to the mastery of data or information about the world. Its appearance in Proverbs usually gives us no clue as to where on the "intimacy spectrum" we should plot any particular usage. Rather than letting that frustrate us, let's use this uncertainty as an invitation to use the word "knowledge" imaginatively in its full Biblical panoply-- unless the text tells us differently.

Four things that are true about knowledge, and our relationship to it, in Proverbs are: (1) one goal of life is to seek it; (2) once we find it we need to store it up; (3) it becomes its own reward; and (4) it is easy to obtain for the discerning person.

1. Seeking Knowledge.

The Book of Proverbs makes no distinction between knowledge sought "as an end in itself," as we might say, and knowledge as a "means to an end." That kind of distinction rests on our unexamined philosophical assumptions about utility and worth of information in the world. When students used to ask me insistently, "Dr. Long, what will be on the test?" or "What do I have to know to do well on the test?" I would do two things. I would, actually, prepare a study sheet for them so that they could be prepared for the exam but then, before I distributed it, I would gently chide them. Why? Because of their limited vision. How can you really say what kind of knowledge you *need* to do well on an exam? Perhaps a quotation from Lincoln or Oliver Wendall Holmes, Jr. would actually illumine an issue that someone was trying to address in contract law. Maybe a historical allusion to a person, act or other thing might throw light on a concept in insurance law. My concern was that if they looked at their school life as a *knowledge-limiting* life, they would be tempted to look at their work life in that way. Their intellectual horizons might not only be dimmed, but they might also miss out on all kinds of work that would only come their way because they sought knowledge. As a teacher, then, I saw myself primarily as one who stimulated a quest for knowledge.

The philosophy of Proverbs agrees with this approach, and it anchors the quest for knowledge in both theological and secular terms. On the one hand, the verses quoted at the beginning of this essay say nothing about the theological underpinnings of knowledge. We are simply told that the mind of one who has understanding seeks knowledge or that an intelligent mind acquires knowledge. Actually, the word for "mind" in 18:15 is the Hebrew word *leb*, which is best translated "heart." Literally, then, we have: "An insightful heart acquires knowledge, and the ear of the wise seeks knowledge." But then, on the other hand, Prov. 2:1-5 urges the seeking of wisdom and understanding so that one would find the "knowledge of God" (2:5). We must conclude, then, that the urgent search for knowledge, driven by the understanding heart, is the cornerstone of attaining further wisdom. Knowledge is wisdom's fuel. Wisdom, then, doesn't just consist of abstruse ruminations on gossamer subjects; it is deeply anchored to the practical realities of knowledge mastery.

2. Storing Up Knowledge.

So, we set our hearts to seek knowledge. Proverbs assures us that we will find it. There is a little bit of a "chicken and egg" problem here (i.e., you seem to have to desire knowledge to get it, but knowledge is a prerequisite to get the desire for it), but a different chicken and different egg exists in every human endeavor. You must love before being able to love; you must have experience to find a job, but you can't get that experience without a job.

Once we find the knowledge of God and the knowledge that is the focus of our quest, we do best to "store it up." Proverbs 10:14 states it this way:

> "The wise lay up knowledge;
>   but the babbling of a fool brings ruin near."

The Hebrew verb translated "lay up" (*zaphan*) doesn't appear frequently in the Bible, but it generally means to "store up" or "to store securely" or to "hide or conceal for a definite purpose."[3] The idea is that one treasures what one stores up. Psalm 119:11 gives an illuminating usage:

> "I treasure (verb is *zaphan*) your word in my heart,
>   so that I may not sin against you."

---

3   Waltke, Bruce, *The Book of Proverbs*, vol. 1, p. 220.

Why do we lay it up? Two reasons. First, so that you will be able to draw upon the treasure when you need it, such as to answer someone or to use it for your own benefit, or, second, so that you might be able to answer the fool. Proverbs. 10:14 is clear on this. By contrasting the laying up of knowledge to the babbling of the fool, Proverbs points to the "toxic" nature of the fool's speech. Only a heart committed to knowledge, knowledge that is stored up and treasured, can fully answer the fool.

Storing up knowledge can be done in very practical ways. The best way I know is to develop a system for two things: (1) to remind me of what I have learned and (2) to enable me to "move knowledge" from the notebook to the memory. The specifics of knowledge acquisition, retention and recall are beyond the scope of this chapter, but they are form the basis of another book I am writing.[4]

3. Knowledge as Reward

Knowledge serves as a crown or diadem for those who pursue it. Notice Proverbs 14:18,

> "The simple are adorned with folly,
> but the clever are crowned with knowledge."

A better translation of the first colon of 14:18 is "the simple *inherit* folly." Thus, the verse is really about inheritances, or what we in law call "trusts and estates." The simple, instead of getting a plush estate and all the trimmings, end up inheriting folly. The simple, in Proverbs, are "fools in training." They haven't yet reached the plateau of folly, but they are in danger of reaching it every day. If they continue in their simplicity, folly is their

---

4   Tentatively titled: *Teaching and Learning in America: 2010.*

result, their inheritance. In contrast, the clever (*arumim*), who are a form or species of the wise, are crowned with knowledge. If knowledge wasn't so important for the author, it would never be the reward which adorns us.

4. The Ease of Knowledge.

Finally, and possibly to our surprise, knowledge acquisition is easy. We often think that gaining knowledge is nothing but hard work, relentless and unforgiving toil, and frequent bouts of forgetfulness and partial understanding. But Proverbs 14:6 assures us,

> "A scoffer seeks wisdom in vain,
>> but knowledge is easy for one who understands."

I suppose one might say, "well, you have to 'understand' first," but that is the basic "chicken and egg" problem mentioned above. Once you commit yourself to the way of learning, of understanding, of knowledge, of wisdom, you find that knowledge acquisition becomes easier and easier all the time. The word translated "easy" is *naqal*, derived from the verb *qalal*, whose most vivid use in the Hebrew Bible is in II Kings 3:18. In that passage a trio of kings, from Israel, Judah and Edom, set out to bring King Mesha of Moab to book for repudiating his duties to the King of Israel. They marched for seven days to find Mesha, but then ran out of water. They say,

> "Alas! The Lord has summoned us, three kings,
>> only to be handed over to Moab," II Kings 3:10.

When the prophet Elisha was called for assistance, a frequent occurrence in those days, he said,

> "This [i.e, filling your need for water] is only a trifle
> (*naqal*) in the sight of the Lord…" II Kings 3:18.

That is how easy knowledge is for the discerning one. A snap. A trifle. I am developing a method for "easy" knowledge acquisition, which can be used by students of all disciplines. In the meantime, however, dedicate yourself to the path of learning today. Soon you will be setting up notebooks and filing systems to make sure that all your insights are preserved. It will, as Proverbs assures us, lead to all kinds of new insights:

> "Then you will understand righteousness and justice
>   and equity, every good path,
>   for wisdom will come into your heart,
>   and knowledge will be pleasant to your soul,"
>   2:9-10.

Day Twenty

AN EXAMPLE OF KNOWLEDGE ACQUISITION

LET ME TELL YOU A STORY of knowledge acquisition, acquisition which was "easy" for me (Proverbs 14:6) and which resulted in some rich insights into history, theology, family relationships and wisdom. It also deepened a relationship I have with a friend. Well, my friend is named Katherine Hart, born in 1924, who lives in the same house in which she was born in Garden City, KS. To be sure, she left home when she went to college in Colorado. When she returned after college she and her husband lived in a different house to raise their four daughters. But when her parents died in the 1980s and 1990s, she moved back to her girlhood home. I start my story with her in her home, figuratively speaking, because it indicates something lovely about Katherine — she has a unique pride in her own family history. It is as if she still communes with her ancestors in the night.

One day, when I was visiting her in her office (she still works full-time and runs an office), she showed me one of the products of her family history. It was an "Album," originally a blank book of approximately 50 or so leaves and about 6" x 9" in size. The Album was given by her great-great grandfather, Dr. Abiel Moore Caverly, to his future bride, Caroline Ames, in 1844. Such a book is similar to the school yearbook in our day, though without photos. Friends write inspiring, or sometimes amusing, things in it. Abiel's Album book for Caroline had several messages written in it. It turned out that Abiel and Caroline were married the next year, but she died unexpectedly in 1851, without any children. Abiel married again and had two children later in the 1850s and 1860s, from one of whom my friend is descended.

TURNING TO THE ALBUM

When Katherine showed me the Album, I wanted to find everything about it I could. I wanted to see if this Album could be my avenue into insight, if possible, into a family, another time, and into the ideas that were written to Caroline Ames late in 1844. The only thing the Album said by way of identification for the publisher was "J & C Riker New York." There were several pictures in the Album, covered over by diaphanous tissue paper; one of them said only "Caldwell's Landing." My first thought was that this "Landing/water" picture had to be of the Hudson River because of its centrality to American life at that period. So I began searching. Sure enough, there was a John C. Riker, who produced many of these Albums, often for commemorative events, out of several business addresses in Brooklyn and Manhattan from the 1830s-1850s. Indeed, one web site introduces us to John C. Riker's work and cites as an example the fine commemorative Album he did in 1857 for the laying of the Atlantic Cable.[1]

I began to devour the web page, learning about Riker's style, the purpose of Albums, the evolution of his career, etc. I learned that a substantial collection of these Albums is housed in the American Antiquarian Society in Worcester, MA. The design on the cover of my friend's "Riker" Album was similar in style to those shown on the web site. All of a sudden I was thrown back in time 165 years to the times when people gave these Albums as presents to each other to commemorate important events or to hope for one in the future (as Abiel hoped to marry Caroline).

I felt, however, that I had only begun my quest. What was "Caldwell's Landing?"[2] Well, I found the same engraving that appeared in the Album by doing a simple web search, and realized that the picture was published in a book in 1840 and then used by Riker (Did copyright protection have to be secured? Did Riker have to ask for permission to use it? How much did he pay for it?). I realized that the dark and mysterious Hudson River scenes were reflective of the time, and I wondered how the deep influence of Washington Irving and other early 19th century NY writers might have evoked a romantic view of the Hudson River among artists. Indeed, I recalled that the Hudson River School of American painting was flourishing about this time, with Thomas Cole and others leading the way.

GOING DEEPER

So, this little "book Album" was produced in the early 1840s, and I could tell my friend something about Riker, about

---

1   http://atlantic-cable.com/Album/riker.htm

2   The picture is here: http://www.texaschapbookpress.com/magellanslog91/americanlandscapeengravings05.htm

the nature of Albums at this time and the engraving that was in the book. But then, there was more. I began to look at the wording of Abiel's long message to Caroline, written in his stable hand in 1844. He was 27 at the time, having graduated from medical school and begun a practice in Loudon VT. By the end of his life in 1879 he had written two significant works of history (the histories of the two towns: Troy, New Hampshire and Pittsford, Vermont where he spent his professional career), histories which still are quoted today. I was fascinated by reading the words that he sent to Caroline. Recall that he was "courting" her by giving her this present in 1844. Well, he began by stating his admiration for her but, before long, he descended into the most interesting and, to us, irrelevant theological discourse. He talked about the vanities of life, the temptations and pains to which we mortals are subject, and then grounded it all in the sin of our first parents in the Garden of Eden. For the next page or so he couldn't stop talking about the trials of this mortal existence. I was amazed. Is this the way that a prominent country doctor normally would have tried to win his way into a young woman's heart in Vermont in the mid-1840s?

But then I found myself asking other questions. Why would someone have found a narrative like this persuasive or instructive? Certainly if someone had written such a statement to his intended in the 1650s in the Massachusetts Bay Colony, one could have understood it. But how how long did the rather rigid Calvinism evinced in Abiel's words still meet with approbation? Those who have studied the history of American religion know that the customary account of the decline of Calvinism in New England claims that it happened right after Independence or perhaps, at latest, in the first or second decade of the 19th century. But here we have a robust Calvinism in an educated man well into the 5th decade of the century. While I marveled at the words, I marveled more that they gave me an insight into the persistence of a certain brand of Congregationalism that lasted far longer than we might have expected.

Then, I decided to step back for a moment and consider the names in the Album. Abiel is one of those Biblical names so popular in 17th and 18th centuries in New England. But the general theory on the more obscure Old Testament names is that they had faded by about 1750 or, at the latest, 1800. The democratic spirit of the American revolution (1776-1783) was supposed to have resulted in more "democratic" names, such as Charles, William, Richard or George. Biblical names like Abiel or Israel or Hezekiah were so popular in the 17th and 18th centuries because they reflected the people's belief that they were the "New Israel," a "chosen people" to head into the howling wilderness of New England. But here again it was different. Abiel was born in 1817, with the "obscure" name. Yet things changed in his family in the next generation. Charles, born in 1856, was Abiel's only son. Old Testament names were no longer the order of the day. By the way, Abiel's father, Solomon (a more famous biblical name than Abiel, to be sure) was born in 1795.

Well, the more I looked at matters, the more they seemed to yield secrets to me. I learned that Abiel and Solomon, father and son, actually died within 4 1/2 months of each other in 1879. Abiel was an indefatigable doctor, and he fell sick after a house call and quickly died at age 62. His father was 84. What must young Charles, then also an aspiring doctor at age 23, have felt to have lost two generations of mentors so quickly? Then I realized that Charles Caverly would be a "star" in his own right, for he would later become a member of the Vermont state board of health, to whom a posthumous volume on infantile paralysis in Vermont was dedicated in 1924.

CONCLUSION

As I was discovering these things I realized that they were just the beginnings of some rich insights into the lives of my friend's ancestors, but that they also opened the world of mid-19th century Vermont in ways that no textbook could have done. A simple Album started me on my quest for knowledge, and by the next day I had considerably deepened my understanding of theology, history, my friend's family, a bit of the history of medicine and the vagaries and sadness of human existence. My life, and that of others, will be enriched because of this knowledge quest. And, in fact, this knowledge quest and discovery is indeed a part of the wisdom quest of which Proverbs speaks, for anything that leads to deeper appreciation of the human condition as well as humbles us with our insularity and relative ignorance, has to be the first step in wisdom.

It is that kind of knowledge that Proverbs encourages. Is it knowledge "for its own sake?" I don't know the meaning of those words in quotation marks. It was knowledge eagerly sought and greatly appreciated and delightfully absorbed and gladly told. Where will your knowledge quests lead *you*?

Day Twenty-One

WISDOM, PROVERBS 19:2-3 AND FALSE STARTS IN LIFE

"Desire without knowledge is not good
> and one who moves too hurriedly misses the way.
One's own folly leads to ruin,
> yet the heart rages against the Lord," Prov. 19:2-3

INTRODUCTION

WE OFTEN THINK OF PROVERBS as a collection of moral aphorisms or pieces of practical advice to the young and those who would like to become wise. We further assume that the advice is clearly stated, easily applied and readily measured. What we are not prepared for in Proverbs is the subtlety of psychological probing throughout the book. For example, as we have seen, 14:10 has:

> "The heart knows its own bitterness,
>   and no stranger shares its joy."

Or, take 15:13,

> "A glad heart makes a cheerful countenance,
>   but by sorrow of heart the spirit is broken."

Both of these verses, and many more, encourage us to see Proverbs not just as a collection of pithy pieces of memorable advice but also as a sort of fine surgical instrument capable of making deep insertions into our hearts. *Proverbs probes*. Perhaps that should be the "bumper sticker" coming from this book.

Proverbs 19:2-3 are among the sharpest of the probing instruments in the surgical kit of the book. The 17 Hebrew words of 19:2-3 give us the "life cycle" or "biography" of millions of young and not so young people who set out on the path of life with eagerness but soon fail and are unable to pick themselves up from their losses. In very few words these verses pierce the heart of those who would be wise, make us consider our past, and leave us with the choice of how we now will live.

UNDERSTANDING THE FLOW OF 19:2-3

The words of 19:2-3 are as choppy in Hebrew as the broken life they intend to describe. Hebrew phrases can often be rendered in more than one way, and conjunctions are no exception to the rule, but let's make an attempt to give a literal translation of the verses.

"Also (still) a desire (or appetite) without knowledge
is not good
and (or thus) hastening with the legs misses the
mark.
Foolishness of a person overthrows his way
and (or yet) against God his heart rages."

The first two cola speak of ways we pursue the quests of life. Each one of us who is gifted with ambition is driven by some kind of desire. Desire, in fact, can often be the overriding reality in our lives. I recall the days of my youth, when I was so driven by longing, by yearning, by a desire to see things happen through my power or insight or God's work in my life that I could almost *taste* the success for which I longed. If Jesus said, upon clearing the Temple of money-changers, "Zeal for thy house will consume me," I could easily have said the same thing to God— zeal for your glory, or my success, is eating me up.

Yet Proverbs probes behind the desire and tells us that desire without knowledge is not a good thing. But surely, I say to myself, for many years, I pursued my desires with knowledge, didn't I? I prayed for my life, for others. I committed each day to God. I lived ethically, to the best of my ability. I so much wanted God's glory to be manifest in the world through my longing and effort. Yet Proverbs doesn't let me, or you, get away with that glib answer. All it says is that desire without knowledge isn't good. It makes us wonder whether, in fact, we have lived lives of desire without knowledge.

As I think back on my life, I see that I wasn't able to "hear" verse 2 for more than 20 years after I began my career in 1982. But then, a few years ago, I began to still the inner protests in my life and confess, "Yes, God, I was driven by desire, to be sure, but now I know it wasn't a particularly focused desire or good one. I didn't sit down and think. I rushed. I felt I had to hustle, to make contacts, to write articles, to be promoted, to do all the things that consume an ambitions person. It was not a desire informed by knowledge."

In fact, the second line of the text describes my life pretty well from about 1982-86. I hastened. I hastened with all my heart, committing myself to too many things, saying "yes" to too many people, running on empty too much of the time, ignoring the cries of my family and loved ones to take things a little more slowly, feeling that I had to reach certain milestones by a certain time or else my life would irreversibly fail and be over. But I know now that I hastened and missed the mark. I was given what you might call "four years of grace" by God from 1982-86 to pursue a life on many fronts. I had many "successes" in that time as a young Assistant Professor. But I never savored a triumph; I never cautiously built a life. I took one victory as a sign that I needed two more very quickly. And I hastened and missed the mark.

PERSONAL REFLECTIONS

Let us assume that someone would have stopped me in 1985 or early 1986, before my "losses" began to accumulate, and said to me, "Bill, you are driven by such desire, but this desire is only forcing you to act hastily. You are not savoring your life and the lessons coming your way. You are not taking the time you need to care for yourself and others. You, in fact, are living a reckless life which will end up disappointing you." What would I have responded (by the way, I have no memory of anyone saying this to me; perhaps I couldn't even *hear* people..) to such a person?

I would have thanked him or her, demonstrating a geniality and kindness that characterized me at the time, but would have thought deeply that this person really doesn't know what s/he is saying. Why? Because the person really doesn't know *me*. In fact, I thought, in my haste and arrogance, the person really *can't* know me.

Thus, I went on, compiling an ever-more impressive resume, making sure that everything I did went into it, trying to energize every group I attended, entertaining the notion that I was bringing special light to the world. I now know I was living a life characterized by self-deception and arrogance. I now know it was the life described, in about 10 words, in Proverbs 19:2.

THE JUDGMENT AND HOPE OF PROVERBS 19:3

Now we are ready for Proverbs 19:3. All it says it "the foolishness of a man (person) overthrows him (her)." The Hebrew verb translated "overthrows" (*salap*) is particularly strong here; it only occurs seven times in the Bible, four of which are in Proverbs. An example is:

"Righteousness guards one whose way is upright,
but sin overthrows (*salap*) the wicked," 13:6.

That is, the verb is elsewhere in Proverbs associated with the utter ruin of the wicked or foolish. So in 19:3 it is "foolishness" which overthrows a person. The first word of 19:3 ("foolishness") summarizes, in one word, the person who acted in 19:2—the person who acted with more desire than knowledge, the person who acted with haste. Such a person is, simply, a foolish person. And, I came to realize, that was what I was. My "professional" haste began in 1982, my distress began in 1986, and both continued for many a year thereafter. Before and after 1986 I would have been loathe to admit that I was a fool. In fact, I was quite proud of myself; I just couldn't figure out what went wrong and why everything of significance in my life seemed to be falling apart. I couldn't really recognize myself as a fool until about 18-20 years after my distress began.

What did I do in the meantime? Well, what does the rest of 19:3 say? "Yet against God his/her heart rages." I did exactly that. My favorite Biblical book from 1986-2005 was the Book of Job. I wrote three books on it and published more than 100 essays on my web site on Job. It was the most blessed book to me in life. I studied it, memorized it, internalized it, prayed every prayer that Job prayed in it. In fact, it energized me in my own anger against God. Job was convinced in his distress that God actually hated him. I didn't go that far, but I became pretty cynical about God's power and, ultimately, about God's existence. If, I argued, God is so good, and I have *tried so hard* to do things right, why is *everything* consistently falling apart for me? My writing relationships weren't working; my marriage didn't work; my "career" was moving in fits and starts as I raged against God. I was still pretty good at concealing the rage, but underneath I was a man who had given up hope. The words of Proverbs 17:22 summed up my life:

> "A cheerful heart is a good medicine,
>   but a downcast spirit dries up the bones."

I was inconsolable. Again, Proverbs described my condition exactly:

"The human spirit will endure sickness;
  but a broken spirit—who can bear?" 18:14.

One of my favorite verses in those days was Job 17:11,

"My days are past, my plans are broken off,
  the desires of my heart."

So, I was in the precise position envisioned by Proverbs 19:2-3. I set out boldly on my career, armed with an Ivy League Ph. D. and study at a leading European university. I hastened in everything I did. I was consumed with mammoth desires for success. I characterized it with the rubric of helping others or teaching others, but it was motivated by my desire to succeed— big time. After four years, beginning in 1986, I was overthrown. I faced six major setbacks in the next three years. I didn't realize at the time that it was my foolishness, foolishness that consisted of hasty running and unchecked desire, that overthrew me. Because I didn't understand this, I simply raged against God. I justified my rage because it gave me a great occasion to master the Book of Job. Yet I was inconsolable for years and, I am afraid, became harder and harder to live with in that time.

CONCLUSION

It was not until the last few years that I realized I had been living and acting, in large measure, as a fool. Many people are able to identify their foolishness and gradually move out of it. It took me about 20 years to do so. I was able to move away from foolishness when I abandoned my pretensions and expectations, and realized that the blows I suffered were meant to be kindly blows to bring me to humility rather than lead me to rage. For years I had taken them as blows of a foe rather than from a loving God that wanted to bring me back to fellowship with Him. But when I started seeing things differently, I was able to be calm and look carefully and cautiously at life. And so, I gave up the Book of Job. And I picked up Proverbs. And, in my surprise, I found my life in Proverbs. But this time it didn't take me 42 chapters, as in Job, fully to understand it. I realized my life was summarized in about 17 words in Prov. 19:2-3. And that has made all the difference.

Day Twenty-Two
LOVING DISCIPLINE—ABOUT TWENTY MINUTES LATER

IT IS AMAZING HOW LONG it takes some of us to learn basic but crucial lessons of life. How long has it taken to learn self-control? To learn patience? To learn how to pummel our pride and simply accept defeat graciously? To perceive when it is time for us to leave and move on to something else? To learn how to love and express our emotions in love? To learn how to believe in ourselves and trust our instincts?

The Book of Proverbs is convinced that one of the most important, and perhaps one of the most difficult, lessons for the wise person to learn is how to accept discipline and instruction, how to receive rebuke and counsel. The ideal wise person "loves" these things, but the title of this essay expresses what I consider to be the more realistic attitude towards correction or discipline. We receive correction, and *want* to love it but the pain of the discipline is such that the sting doesn't really "wear off" until about 20 minutes later. As the Scriptures say, "For the moment, all discipline seems painful...," Hebrews 12:11.

If there is an iconic individual who personifies the commitment to one form of discipline--physical discipline--over a life's course it is the fitness guru Jack LaLanne. Born in 1914, he is still going strong at his 95th birthday, the time of this writing. His claims to fame involve starting the "workout gym" model in the 1930s, doing "camera-catching" feats of physical prowess, such as dragging huge boats across large bodies of water with his teeth while manacled, performing steady and demanding physical workouts, and practicing an uncompromising diet. Even at 95 he says he works out more than two hours a day, though the intensity of workouts has, of course, declined. When interviewed on one occasion, he was asked whether he loved working out, since he did it so much. His response startled me, "I hate it," he said. Yet surely the fruit of the workout is his pleasure. He loves the discipline—twenty minutes later.

The goal of this chapter is to have us become "Jack LaLanne's of wisdom," or, more prosaically, to become people who know how to embrace and even love, the process and fruit of verbal, rather than physical, discipline. In order to do this I will briefly examine three topics which present ever-more-difficult kinds of discipline or instruction to accept: (1) seeking and receiving counsel; (2) responding to instruction and correction; (3) handling rebuke. I will begin the chapter by contrasting how the wise and foolish react differently to instruction.

INSTRUCTION, REPROOF AND THE WISE AND FOOLISH/SCOFFER

The Book of Proverbs has four main terms for the subject of this chapter. They are usually rendered in English as "discipline, admonition, instruction or rebuke." Three of these can be used interchangeably (*musar*, instruction or discipline; *tokahat*, admonition or reproof; *etsah*, counsel) and one of which stands by itself (*gearah*, rebuke). Together they emphasize that one of the basic realities of life for a wise person is growth in wisdom, growth that often comes through the instrumentality of correction by others.

Proverbs is aware that a signal difference between the wise and foolish in how they relate to correction.

> "Whoever corrects a scoffer wins abuse;
>> whoever rebukes the wicked gets hurt.
> A scoffer who is rebuked will only hate you;
>> The wise, when rebuked, will love you.
> Give instruction to the wise, and They will become
>> wiser still;
>> Teach the righteous and they will gain in
>> learning," 9:7-9.

Scoffers, a subset of the fool, hate correction because of their pride. They have little self-knowledge and consequently believe that they have the key or answer to a situation. Attempted correction yields only hatred and scorn. Perhaps the scoffer or fool can externally conceal their scorn for the one who corrects, but the scoffer will vilify, crucify and try to obliterate that person in their mind.

In contrast, a wise person, when corrected or rebuked, will love the one doing the rebuking. Why? Because the wise person, fundamentally, loves knowledge and learning, and has the maturity and insight to know that correction is a means by which he or she grows in knowledge. Responding to correction means that you have to leave your perspective to the side for a moment while you respond to or try to understand the correction of another. You have to know how to still or quiet your emotions. You need to be able to listen to another. You need to be able to evaluate the other, even if you aren't able to sort out precisely what they are saying because of their tone, clarity or understanding. And, you need to live your life slightly differently as a result of the correction. To respond wisely to correction, and not to try to ward it off through self-defensive maneuvers, takes all the wisdom we can muster—and, indeed, maybe *more* than we can muster.

ADVICE AND COUNSEL

A consistent message in Proverbs is that the wise person seeks advice.

"Without counsel, plans go wrong,
but with many advisers they succeed," 15:22.

One of the things I do in life other than write books and study a lot is to counsel people and corporate bodies who are engaging in significant life or business changes. What is clear to me is that people facing significant changes, either thrust upon them or chosen freely, need counsel. I ask them for their "plans." They often respond in a way that makes me see their plans are, in fact, in shambles. Often they don't know how to get "from here to there." They don't realize that there are dozens of things to do, most quite easy and practical, before they can reach their goals or even feel good about their work. Indeed, my counseling relationship with people in these situations sometimes exposes vulnerabilities that people never knew they had, as well as helps them focus on skills and desires which they also hadn't quite identified. Yet, if they didn't engage in this guided process, they certainly would "go wrong."

The Scriptures tell us that we are wonderfully and curiously made. One characteristic of us is that we cannot really live by ourselves. We need others to function well. Even the most isolated survivalist or most dedicated anchorite (solitary monk) needs the weapons of his trade, whether they be military or spiritual assault weapons. Yet, as we become more and more skilled at something, the myth of independence tends to take over our psyche. We *think* we need no one's help. We trust our own instincts fully. We have confidence in our mind alone.

Proverbs is wiser than that. It recognizes the central importance of advisors to help us realize our plans. This is also true in the wider political process.

> "Where there is no guidance, a nation falls,
>> but in an abundance of counselors there is
>> safety," 11:14.

Lest we miss the connection between advice and wisdom, we have:

> "By insolence the heedless make strife,
>> but wisdom is with those who take advice," 13:10.

Perhaps the problem with some of us is that we listen to advice but have no judgment regarding who is giving us the best advice or good advice. Proverbs is not unaware of the conundrum of human trust, but is quite convinced that abundance of counselors will help us. Why? Because Proverbs always anchors or grounds our trust desires with a trust in God:

> "Trust in the Lord in with all your heart,
>   and do not rely on your own insight.
> In all your ways acknowledge him,
>   And he will make straight your paths," 3:5-6.

REPROOF AND CORRECTION

Reproof, correction, discipline, admonition and instruction are a constellation of terms used by translators of the three Hebrew words cited above to express the variety of means of correcting a person. Often the terms *musar* and *tokahat* are linked, as in the following verses:

> "And you say, 'Oh, how I hated discipline,
>   and my heart despised reproof!," 5:12.

> "Whoever heeds instruction is on the path to life
>   but one who rejects a rebuke goes astray," 10:17.

> "A fool despises a parent's instruction,
>   but one who heeds admonition is prudent," 15:5.

> "Those who ignore instruction despise themselves,
>   but those who heed admonition gain
>   understanding," 15:32.

Thus, we can understand the concept of discipline or instruction or reproof or admonition as including all the ways that people (or God), authoritative or casual, try to bring correction into our lives. This kind of correction can sting; it can momentarily cloud the vision; it can evoke bitter or charged reactions. It rarely is greeted with effusive gratitude. It is almost too hard for us to accept. That is why Proverbs tells us:

"My child, do not despise the Lord's discipline
    or be weary of his reproof,
for the Lord reproves the one he loves,
    as a father the son in whom he delights," 3:11-12.

The biggest challenge that many face in life is to accept the distresses in life as gifts from God, either directly given or through the instrumentality of others, for us to get a heart of wisdom. Wisdom is the gift of pain, if we let the pain work its way at its own pace through our system.

Nor should we, who aspire to wisdom, decline the role of being the one who corrects others.

"Whoever rebukes a person will afterward find more
    favor
than one who flatters with the tongue," 28:23.

One of the reasons I left teaching after two decades at it in a variety of higher education contexts is that I had what I would call a "crisis of correction." I didn't know how I should correct students. Should I correct their grammar when speaking? When writing? Should I only criticize their ideas? Should I engage in lengthy encounters with them, pointing out weaknesses as well as strengths? Should I simply affirm their ideas when they are good? Should I ask them how they wanted to be corrected? To what extent is a relationship a prerequiste of correction? Or, can correction just be assumed because of the student/teacher role? I would say that many of my colleagues have been wrestling with the same ideas; I come at it from the perspective of Proverbs. Correction, for a wise person, is a very useful thing; correction for a fool only brings you enmity.[1]

THE NOTION OF REBUKE

The word translated "rebuke" is only used twice in Proverbs (*gearah*), even though many English translations of Proverbs use the word "rebuke" to translate other Hebrew terms. As Waltke[2] and others say, *gearah* is a term to express correction *with moral indignation*. That is, it is a very strong form of correction, a sort of "you did what??!!" response. The two texts where it appears are here:

"A wise child loves discipline
>but a scoffer does not listen to rebuke (*gearah*),"
>>13:1.

"A rebuke (*gearah*) strikes deeper into a discerning
>person
>than a hundred blows into a fool," 17:10.

The term can be used to describe the great and forceful power which God directed at primeval chaos or waters:

---

1   One form of correction that I am not dealing with in this book is corporal correction. The Book of Proverbs is not averse to it; it even advises it (13:25; 23:13-14).
2   *The Book of Proverbs, 1-15*, p. 551.

"Then the channels of the sea were seen,
        and the foundations of the world were laid bare,
at your rebuke, O Lord,
        at the blast of the breath of your nostrils," Ps.
        18:15.

"Thus says the Lord....
    Why was no one there when I came?
Why did no one answer when I called?
    Is my hand shortened, that it cannot redeem?
Or have I no power to deliver?
    By my rebuke I dry up the sea...," Is. 50:2.

But it can also refer to God's reaction to moral shortcomings:

"Your children have fainted,
        they lie at the head of every street
like an antelope in a net;
        they are full of the wrath of the Lord,
        the rebuke of your God," Is. 51:20.

Proverbs 17:10 explores how a wise person reacts to this kind of moral indignation. A *gearah* goes more deeply into her or him than 100 blows into a fool. The wise person has developed a deep conscience or soul, and is very conscious, almost hyper-aware, of its own shortcomings and weaknesses. When moral fault is rightly pointed out, it slices to the heart of the wise person. The only response is, like Peter, to go out and weep (Luke 22:61-62) or, with David, to say, "I have sinned against the Lord," II Sam. 12:13. Indeed, David's response to Nathan's words to him in II Sam 12, regarding his dalliance with Bathsheba in II Sam 11, is first to get angry (II Sam. 12:5) and then to be ashamed of himself. The wise person not only takes correction with grace, but admits, sometimes almost shamefully, a moral failure.

CONCLUSION

There is no better word to close our chapter than a simple proverb:

"Listen to advice and accept instruction,
that you may gain wisdom for the future," 19:20.

Let us hope that someday, maybe very soon, this would become easy for us (cf. Prov. 14:6).

Day Twenty-Three

WISDOM AND THE STRENGTH OF HUMILITY

INTRODUCTION—A WORD ON PRIDE

APART FROM THE TOPIC of wealth and poverty, there are few subject treated in Proverbs with more care than pride and humility. The scoffer or mocker, whom we met in Day 12, is characterized as one who "acts with arrogant pride," 21:24. The *Oxford English Dictionary* defines pride as: "A high, esp. an excessively high, opinion of one's own worth or importance which gives rise to a feeling or attitude of superiority over others; inordinate self-esteem."[1] John Milton, the great English-language poet of the Christian epic, used the word this way:

> "Vain hopes, vain aimes, inordinate desires Blown
> up with high conceits ingendring pride,"
> *Paradise Lost* IV. 809-810.

---

1   *Oxford English dictionary, s.v.*

The only proverb from the Book of Proverbs which still retains much use in 21st century English is about pride:

"Pride goes before destruction,
and a haughty spirit before a fall," 16:18.

And pride (Latin: *superbia*) is listed as one of the seven deadly sins in Medieval Catholicism. The list of the seven sins,[2] derived from a list of eight evil thoughts of a 4th century Christian Bishop, is reminiscent of the list of "six things that the Lord hates, seven things which are an abomination to him" of Proverbs 6:16-19. The only "sin" that is common to all three lists is pride.

Pride, or inordinately high self-esteem, is toxic for two reasons: it blinds a person, and it masks fear. Pride blinds a person in three areas—it makes a person unable to learn, it limits their interpretation of others' actions, and it hinders self-understanding. The proud person focuses on the self and thus isn't really open to the stunning variety of knowledge all around us. A learner must learn, first of all, to still the internal voices and demands in order to listen to what the object teaches. Then, you can integrate the self and our needs to the learning. Pride inverts this process by making learning a study in the exaltation of the self. Because so much care goes to maintaining the image of the self, little understanding of others or the self can follow.

At its root, pride is a reaction of fear. It is a declaration to the world that the proud person doesn't trust the world enough to grant him or the recognition he thinks is due. Because of the sense of wounded honor, of lack of recognition deserved, the proud person lives in fear—fear that the rest of the world can't quite get it right in describing you. Thus, the proud person has

---

2   http://en.wikipedia.org/wiki/Seven_deadly_sins

to spend all her time promoting herself in order to make sure that people have the right interpretive film to lay over her life. The Book of Proverbs has no tolerance for this kind of person; her fall is certain.

THE WAY OF HUMILITY

I call this section the "way" of humility because humility is a path, a journey, a struggle. The author of the Letter to the Hebrews recognized this about Jesus: "He learned obedience through what he suffered," Heb. 5:8. And, the major point I will make here is that knowing that the Hebrew verb *anah*, translated "to be humble," originally meant "to be bent over, to be oppressed, to be laid low," tells us what we need to know about humility. The humble are those who have first had the experience of being bent over, being ground into the ground, being oppressed. While the verb focuses on physical oppression, its linguistic breadth could also include mental affliction.

The humble are those who have taken the journey from being bowed down or oppressed, and have learned to build a life of dignity and honor. It is a life in which a person learns to identify her limits, accept them, and live joyfully and with grace within them.[3] It is the precursor attitude to the fear of the Lord, which itself is the beginning of wisdom (9:10).

That humility is a process can be seen from a few Proverbs.

"The fear of the Lord is instruction in wisdom,
     and humility goes before honor," 15:33.

---

3   Bruce Waltke, *The Book of Proverbs, 1-15*, p. 484.

"Before destruction one's heart is haughty,
    but humility goes before honor," 18:12.

The unreflective, and proud, human way of arranging life is to have honor come early in life, because the proud heart imagines itself to be worthy of it at an early age. Yet the humble heart knows that "it is good for me that I was afflicted, so that I might learn your statutes," Ps. 119:71. The humble heart knows that honor is given, not taken. The humble heart doesn't welcome affliction; indeed, no person in her right mind would do that. But it recognizes that the sweet fruit of affliction, often expressed in the sweetness of our tears, brings humility and wisdom. The Biblical pattern of the humble life is to be afflicted, to recognize one's need and limitations, to fear the Lord (1:7), to get the rudiments of wisdom (9:10), to grow in wisdom (1:5) and, finally, to reap "glory and honor and life," 22:4. The experience of being "bent" by life's struggles is a perfect preparation for us to "bend" or "stoop" through the low door to enter into the fear of the Lord and the way of wisdom.

"A person's pride will bring humiliation,
    but one who is lowly in spirit will obtain honor,"
    29:23.

SHOWING HUMILITY ON A DAILY BASIS

Humility manifests itself in deferring to others when you don't have knowledge of a situation and the other does. Deference brings both vulnerability and the possibility of learning, fruitful communication and precious intimacy. A commonplace example from our daily lives illustrates the point. We meet service and sales people all the time. The former generally wait for you to raise your questions, while the latter raise the issue first about what they think you might "need." In dealing with a service person I have found the following method to be infallibly helpful.

I approach the counter or desk. The "service person" has either just dealt with another customer or is engaged in work. Two worlds are about ready to intersect, and the potential pitfalls facing the coming interaction are mammoth. Thankfully, the other person speaks our language (we hope!). But that person is in her universe, you are in yours, you have a need that may not be within the person's competence to fill, you need to express your need or desire, and you need to have ways of moving the conversation along so that you end up getting what you would like to have.

When the conversation begins, a person who is humble paradoxically realizes that the other, the service person, has needs that first ought to be met before she can help you. The service person has dealt with all kinds of people. The greatest fear of the service person is that you, the stranger, might be hostile. The second greatest fear is that she might not understand what you are trying to say or be unable to break through your limited knowledge frame. A humble person can break through these invisible barriers with a reassuring comment or question. In a normal, but quiet voice, you say, "I am in need of help." Or, "There is something I don't quite understand, and I am wondering if you are the person who can help me." An approach like this immediately relaxes the service person; she wants to do all she can to assist you. Gone are her fears—of your hostility and your inability to express yourself. You are asking for help.

The humble person does not hesitate to express his own vulnerability and limited understanding. There is strength

227

is so expressing it because through a method like the one just suggested, the humble person has created the conditions not only for her questions to be answered but also for the service person to share other relevant information that the inquirer has not even considered. That is, on numerous occasions I have approached a service person in the method just described, and she was so disarmed, apparently, by the method, that she ended up volunteering far more valuable information than I sought. I may have assumed that the only way you could do something was X; she let me know, in the process of answering my question, that another method, Y, will be of more use to me. Thus, humility and vulnerability become the means by which additional knowledge and goodwill is gained. You can see, after several of these encounters, how wisdom indeed, in the words of Proverbs, "is with the humble," 11:2.

APPROACHING LIFE WITH HUMILITY

So how does a humble person live? Not every encounter in life is with a service person. Two verses which get us thinking about this question follow:

> "Do not put yourself forward in the king's presence
>   or stand in the place of the great;
> for it is better to be told, 'Come up here,'
>   than to be put lower in the presence of the
>   noble," 25:6-7.

> "Let another praise you, and not your own mouth—
>   a stranger, and not your own lips," 27:2.

The first verses obviously were written in the context of service at the king's court, but their applicability is much broader than that. Indeed Luke "plays" with the thoughts behind these verses in Luke 14:8-11. The latter passage discusses places of honor at a wedding banquet. The message is that it is better to take the "lower" place in such a context and be invited to join the 'head table' later. Luke then glosses it with a familiar word of Jesus:

> "For all who exalt themselves will be humbled,
> and those who humble themselves will be
> exalted," 14:11.

The second verse is a challenge to the American nostrum that unless you toot your own horn no one will do it for you. That is what we are told in school and work. The "stranger" is someone outside the family; we are exhorted twice not to pump ourselves with lips or mouth. The verse, as Waltke says, "protects against self-deception and flattery."[4] We flatter ourselves by thinking that *now* is the time for the recognition we have long deserved. If we leave it in the stranger's hands, and ultimately leave our life in God's hands, we won't have to worry about maintaining a commitment to something we really can't control anyway—the praise of others. Honor, as mentioned before, must be granted, not demanded.

CONCLUSION

Proverbs insists that the life of humility is the one that brings the true rewards:

---

4   *The Book of Proverbs, 15-31*, p. 374.

"The reward of humility and fear of the Lord
is riches and honor and life," 22:4.

We receive by not going after the thing we will receive.
That is the paradoxical message of humility.

Day Twenty-Four

PROVERBS 19:25 AND THE POWER OF (A BAD) EXAMPLE

"Strike a scoffer, and the simple will learn prudence;
reprove the intelligent, and they will gain
knowledge," 19:25.

I AM WRITING THIS ESSAY just after the deaths of four very visible "celebs" in American culture: Farrah Fawcett, Michael Jackson, Steve McNair and Robert McNamara. Except for high finance, they covered the gamut of the "superceleb" world: TV and movies, music, politics, and sports. I happened to be in Nashville the very day and about three blocks from where Steve McNair, former quarterback for the Tennessee Titans, was killed on July 3, 2009. The news stories are still coming out, but it appears that a young woman with whom he had developed a romantic relationship had bought a gun and killed him and herself. We can speculate on the details of what might have happened; indeed, the airwaves are filled with this speculation.

But what is more important for purposes of this essay is the way that Steve McNair's death was quickly interpreted as a moral lesson. I know this because I was engaging in an activity the other day that I hardly ever do—listen to sports talk radio. I did so because I was caught in a traffic jam, caused by an accident, and felt, you might say, trapped. Thus, I did something that enhanced my sense of helplessness in the world: I listened to sports talk radio. They were talking about Steve McNair and his toughness, great performances on the field and selflessness in the community. The gravelly tone, rough speech, and barely acceptable grammar of the radio host made me smile: they definitely were going for a certain demographic among American listeners, I mused. But then I listened to what he was saying. He spoke of Steve's death, and said, "Man, I don't wanna judge anybody here," but he was interested in how Steve's death was causing a lot of other guys to "break it off" with girlfriends or casual dating situations. That is, "it's time, guys (guys who are married, that is) to stop getting gifts for the girlfriends or mistresses, and to leave those relationships aside." Steve McNair had become a warning signal or reality check to American men, especially to sports-loving men who spend most of their time fantasizing anyway, that they would consider the dangers of possible extra-marital relationships.

The response to Steve McNair's death was reminiscent to me of the media's reaction to the release of the 1987 movie "Fatal Attraction." Starring Michael Douglas as a successful New York attorney (Daniel Gallagher) who has a weekend "fling" with Alex Forrest, played by Glenn Close, the film explores Alex's quick descent into obsession—with Gallagher. What Gallagher saw as a weekend diversion was taken by her as the start of a permanent relationship. Well, you have to see the movie to understand its graphic, gripping, emotionally-draining expose of how an obsession can lead to oppression, demands, and, finally, death. After the movie was released (it was the 2nd highest grossing movie of 1987), I remember several commentators saying that "this was the movie that made husbands drop extra-marital relationships." What had seemed so sweet and fun was now seen as deadly serious. Of course, the Book of Proverbs told us that long ago, but we are much more entranced with seeing the faces and writhing bodies of Michael Douglas and Glenn Close on the screen to get the same message.

RETURNING TO PROVERBS

The Book of Proverbs takes the power of example deadly seriously. Interestingly enough, however, it is the power of bad example, rather than good example, that receives most attention in our culture and in Proverbs. This might seem strange at first, since we are always chiding each other to be "good examples" for children (athletes have felt this pressure for years—doesn't the "NBA Care"?). But it seems we are so constituted that we find the power of bad example compelling, while the power of good example does not make headlines. This is probably because good example teaches the importance of hard things—diligence, patience, picking oneself up after loss, the humdrum "boring" quality of much of daily living. Bad example lets us fantasize, ever so briefly, even as we vow to eliminate the fantasies and harmful actions.

Three passages in Proverbs speak of the power of example. Example is, of course, not the only way we are supposed to learn. Proverbs stresses also the disciplined mastery of wisdom principles, trust in God, learning from nature and from reflection on our own experience. But when it talks about learning by example, it gives one predictable lesson and one unpredictable lesson. Let me begin by quoting the "predictable" one:

"I passed by the field of one who was lazy,
    by the vineyard of a stupid person;
and see, it was all overgrown with thorns;
    the ground was covered with nettles,
    and its stone wall was broken down.
Then I saw and considered it;
    I looked and received instruction.
A little sleep, a little slumber,
    A little folding of the hands to rest,
And poverty will come upon you like a robber,
    And want, like an armed warrior," 24;30-34.

The message is clear. We learn from the example of the lazy person that sloth produces poverty. If we want to avoid poverty, we ought not to be lazy. We need to be diligent. Pretty simple message. But a layer of complexity and intrigue is added with two other passages:

"Strike a scoffer, and the simple will learn prudence;
    reprove the intelligent, and they will gain
    knowledge," 19:25.

"When a scoffer is punished, the simple become wiser;
    when the wise are instructed, they increase in
    knowledge," 21:11."

Here the power of a bad example is given a new twist:

234

scoffers are punished not for the sake of the scoffer but for the sake of the *simple*. You recall that the simple are "fools in training" or, more charitably said, inexperienced people who can possibly go either way — they can become wise or they can fall into folly. The simple live, therefore, in a situation of vulnerability. Exhortation can sometimes help them. Instruction in the way of wisdom is often valuable. Sometimes they even need to be disciplined through beating, according to Proverbs. But we ought not to ignore the power of example to turn them to a more productive life. The scoffer gets beaten, and the simple person learns from this experience. In one passage it says that the simple "become wiser." The other says that they will "learn prudence."

How is it that the experience of witnessing the scoffer's getting punished produces wisdom in the simple? It does so in two ways. First it shows the inevitable connection between unjust living and punishment. The scoffer is one who erodes the values of the community. Scoffers spend time concocting unhelpful schemes. They really are interested in participating only to the extent that it benefits them; they have no concern for those outside themselves. They cannot be reformed, and ultimately they must be driven out of the community. But this proverb indicates that it doesn't necessarily have to be done in secret. It should be a public act of driving them out, so that the simple learn that there is a relationship between the activity of the scoffer and his/her punishment. It might take too long for "nature" or "life" to work out in the life of the scoffer so that the simple can clearly see the message. Thus the "striking" of the scoffer by the wise accelerates a message that nature will eventually teach the scoffer. The simple are supposed to conclude by watching the exclusion of the scoffer, "This is the result of the life of mocking others, of the pursuit of violence, of spreading strife, of being completely self-absorbed."

In passing, we now see why it is clear that a beating is the right thing to give the scoffer but not the wise. One might be tempted to say, "If a beating helps the mocker, why not give the same treatment to the wise?" But Proverbs won't "go" there. Why? Proverbs 17:26 gives us a clue:

"To impose a fine on the innocent is not right,
  or to flog the noble for their integrity."

We don't beat the wise person because it would be an act of injustice. The wise person, the "noble" one, is one who tries to build the community and teach the principles of patience, considered speech, wise precepts to the next generation. The wise tries to live these values in his/her own life. Thus, by beating such a person it would give the impression that the wise needs to be reformed in a significant way. But this isn't true. The wise needs instruction, to be sure. The wise needs to be instructed and ought to welcome reproof (12:1), but the wise can learn from correction or discipline. They don't need to be "spanked." If they were made a public spectacle in this way, it would make onlookers think that justice was not the basic principle of society, since a just society doesn't beat its wise citizens.

Second, the experience of the scoffer's beating produces wisdom in the simple because it instructs them that the wise are the source of their strength. Every inexperienced person gains further insight by associating with certain kinds of people. By punishing the scoffer, the wise send the clear message to the simple that their life, their future, their wisdom lies in association with the wise. As Proverbs says:

"Whoever walks with the wise becomes wise,
　　but the companion of fools suffers harm," 13:20.

In walking along the path of life, one chooses companions. What better lesson for the simple to learn in life than that the wise ought to be their companions? One learns by instruction and by osmosis. One "picks up" principles, conduct, good ways of thinking and of making decisions by associating with wise people.

CONCLUSION

The power of example in these verses is not only directed to the simple. The wise, too, are able to learn from instruction. "When the wise are instructed, they increase in knowledge" (21:11). The only way the wise can increase in knowledge through instruction or correction is that they don't object to it. They receive it. They welcome correction, despite the difficulty of receiving the word that they/we need to improve. One of the purposes of the Book of Proverbs is expressed in the preface to the book:

"Let the wise also hear and gain in learning,
　　and the discerning acquire skill," 1:5.

We gain in learning by our own diligent search but also by being corrected. The Book of Proverbs is a sort of educational tool, one that encourages us to make learning the central purpose of our lives. We "increase in knowledge" not for the sake of the increase but for the sake of the wisdom that we then use to serve others. Wisdom is never conceptualized as a solitary accomplishment or something that is to be used to "wow" another person. It is a gift or skill that has its primary use in the community of faith. There is so much foolishness and mockery "out there" that it takes all of the wise person's insight to be of use to the community.

Thus, discipline is foundational to the life of the wise. It is useful to improve us, the wise, but it also is important to eliminate or punish those who tear down the community. In the final analysis, however, the simple are the big "winners," for through correction of others they have the opportunity to move to wisdom through the works of the wise. Now is the time for all of us to be wise.

Proverbs that are Too Good to Miss

Day Twenty-Five

ABRAHAM LINCOLN AND PROVERBS 25:11

BEGINNING WITH THE SECOND INAUGURAL ADDRESS

"A word fitly spoken is like apples of gold in a setting of silver," 25:11.

FOR MANY YEARS, one of the few underappreciated areas in the study of Abraham Lincoln, the Sixteenth President of the US (1861-65), was his intellectual life in general and his engagement with the ideas of the Bible in specific. This lack was partially redressed a generation ago through William Wolf's work[1] and a chapter in Elton Trueblood's biography of Lincoln[2], but it has recently received fresh scrutiny in Allen Guelzo's masterful *Abraham Lincoln: Redeemer President.*[3] Yet, an exposition

---

1   *The Almost Chosen People: The Religion of Abraham Lincoln* (1963)
2   *Abraham Lincoln: Theologian of American Anguish* (1973), ch. 4.
3   Published in 2000.

of the shaping power of the Bible for Lincoln's political and religious understanding still awaits an eloquent expositor. That is, to date scholars have adequately culled many references from Lincoln's work showing the *esteem* in which Lincoln held the Bible, but fewer have been the attempts to show how the very ideas and structure of the Biblical text *shaped or reinforced* Lincoln's ideas.

If I were to take on such a task, two passages in Lincoln's *oeuvre*, one familiar and one almost unknown, would initially beckon me. The familiar one is from his Second Inaugural Address, delivered March 4, 1865. The brevity of the address belies its deep engagement with theological themes, and especially with the theme of the judgment of God expressed in Jesus' words in Matthew 18:7,

> "Woe unto the world because of offenses! It must needs be that offenses come, but woe to that man by whom the offense cometh."

A full quotation of the relevant passage shows its depth:

> "'Woe unto the world because of offenses; for it must needs be that offenses come, but woe to that man by whom the offense cometh.' If we shall suppose that American slavery is one of those offenses which, in the providence of God, must needs come, but which, having continued through His appointed time, He now wills to remove, and that He gives to both North and South this terrible war as the woe due to those by whom the offense came, shall we discern therein any departure from

those divine attributes which the believers in a living God always ascribe to Him? Fondly do we hope, fervently do we pray, that this mighty scourge of war may speedily pass away. Yet, if God wills that it continue until all the wealth piled by the bondsman's two hundred and fifty years of unrequited toil shall be sunk, and until every drop of blood drawn with the lash shall be paid by another drawn with the sword, as was said three thousand years ago, so still it must be said 'the judgments of the Lord are true and righteous altogether.'"[4]

Patiently working through the difficult language of this quoted section shows that Lincoln is performing an extended "midrash on" or "interpretation of" those words of Jesus. Woe comes to the world because of offenses. Slavery is one such offense. Offenses must come because that is the nature of life, but even if offenses are, in their own way, inevitable, people are still judged by the offenses in their midst. So, American slavery is an offense which received the "woe" of war, a terrible war.

Lincoln's long and tortured question about whether the war, therefore, manifests any "departure" from the ways of a just God must be answered in the negative—no, this was all indicated in the Scripture. God is to be praised, even in the midst of this terrible war. The Scripture is true, and the judgments of God are right. Whatever one might think of Lincoln's exposition, it reflects a deep engagement with the text of Jesus' words, an engagement that was sensitive to the very texture and flow of the words.

---

4   The full text of this speech is at: http://www.bartleby.com/124/pres32.html.

LOOKING AT PROVERBS 25:11

Less well known, or not known at all, is the way that Proverbs 25:11, quoted at the beginning of this essay, functioned for him. It was actually stimulated by a December 1860 correspondence with Alexander Stephens of Georgia.[5] Lincoln and Stephens had been long-time acquaintances, and even friends, as each pursued his political career. Stephens was a Southern "moderate," hoping upon hope that secession would not happen and that Civil War could be averted. By March 1861 he would become Vice-President of the Confederacy and an ardent defender of the South. But before any of this happened, before even South Carolina had begun the secession parade on December 20, 1860, while he was still undecided on which course he would pursue, Stephens wrote to Lincoln as President-elect, asking for clarification of Lincoln's position on slavery. Lincoln responded with a brief note of December 22, 1860. In part Lincoln said:

> "Do the people of the South really entertain fears
> that a Republican administration would, directly, or
> indirectly, interfere with their slaves, or with them,
> about their slaves? If they do, I wish to assure you,
> as once a friend, and still, I hope, not an enemy, that
> there is no cause for such fears."[6]

No doubt appreciative of Lincoln's words, Stephens wrote back, on December 30, using the language of Proverbs 25:11,

---

5   A brief sketch of Stephens life is here: http://en.wikipedia.org/wiki/Alexander_Stephens

6   http://quod.lib.umich.edu/cgi/t/text/text-idx?c=lincoln;cc=lincoln;type=simple;rgn=div1;q1=fitly%20spoken;singlegenre=All;view=text;subview=detail;sort=occur;idno=lincoln4;node=lincoln4%3A250

and urging Lincoln to say these things on a larger scale:

> "Personally, I am not your enemy—far from it;
> and however widely we may differ politically, yet I
> trust we both have an earnest desire to preserve and
> maintain the Union. . . . When men come under the
> influence of fanaticism, there is no telling where
> their impulses or passions may drive them. This
> is what creates our discontent and apprehensions,
> not unreasonable when we see . . . such reckless
> exhibitions of madness as the John Brown raid into
> Virginia, which has received so much sympathy
> from many, and no open condemnation from any of
> the leading members of the dominant party. . . . In
> addressing you thus, I would have you understand
> me as being not a personal enemy, but as one
> who would have you do what you can to save our
> common country. *A word fitly spoken by you now
> would be like `apples of gold in pictures of silver.'* "[7]

In other words, Stephens was appealing to Scripture, using the words of Proverbs 25:11, as an incitement for Lincoln to address the nation clearly and "fitly" on the issue of slavery and the Union.

Stephens was so insistent on this matter because the juggernaut of secession was now in full swing. Directly after 1861 dawned, a series of secessions rocked the nation: Mississippi on January 9, Florida on January 10, Alabama on January 11, Georgia itself on January 19 (though Stephens voted against

7   This letter isn't in the Lincoln papers, but was quoted from the just-cited web source, which itself cites *Recollections of Alexander H. Stephens*, edited by Myrta L. Avary (1910), p. 60.

the motion to secede), Louisiana on January 26 and Texas on February 1. January 1861, then, saw the collapse of any hope that the most optimistic Unionist entertained that regional conflict could be avoided.

But still Stephens' words rung in Lincoln's ear. As has been shown by the distinguished Lincoln scholar Merrill Peterson, Lincoln had the habit of focusing on only a few great issues of central importance to him and coming back to those ideas time after time.[8] Two of his "great ideas" were the fact that slavery was inherently wrong and that the concept of liberty for all was enshrined in the basic documents of our national faith (the Declaration of Independence and Constitution) and therefore must be honored above all.

Perhaps because of the perception that the moment that Stephens had appealed to on December 30 had passed, but that the reference to Proverbs 25:11 was still appropriate, Lincoln wrote a "Fragment on the Constitution and the Union," probably sometime in January 1861, on the subject of liberty for all—and Proverbs 25:11. He wrote:

> "Without the Constitution and the Union, we
> could not have attained the result; but even these, are
> not the primary cause of our great prosperity. There
> is something back of these, entwining itself more
> closely about the human heart. That something, is
> the principle of ``Liberty to all''—the principle that
> clears the path for all—gives hope to all—and, by
> consequence, enterprise, and industry to all.
> The expression of that principle, in our
> Declaration of Independence, was most happy, and

---

8   Merrill D. Peterson, *This Grant Pertinacity* (1991).

fortunate. Without this, as well as with it, we could
have declared our independence of Great Britain;
but without it, we could not, I think, have secured
our free government, and consequent prosperity.
No oppressed people will fight, and endure, as our
fathers did, without the promise of something better,
than a mere change of masters."[9]

But how does this central principal of "liberty to all,"
which was interpreted by the South as a sort of "code word"
for abolition of slavery and an indication of the hardening of
positions between North and South, relate to Proverbs 25:11?
Let's read on:

> The assertion of that principle, at that time, was
> the word, "fitly spoken" which has proved an "apple
> of gold" to us. The Union, and the Constitution, are
> the picture of silver, subsequently framed around it.
> The picture was made, not to conceal, or destroy the
> apple; but to adorn, and preserve it. The picture was
> made for the apple—not the apple for the picture.
> So let us act, that neither picture, or apple shall
> ever be blurred, or bruised or broken."[10]

Lincoln's use of Proverbs 25:11 gives us a window into
his mind. He weighs the principle, Liberty for All, a principle
of utmost importance to him since the passage of the Nebraska-

---

9   The citation is from Lincoln's *Collected Works*, vol. IV, pp 168-69,
which appears on the web as :   http://quod.lib.umich.edu/cgi/t/text/text-
idx?c=lincoln;cc=lincoln;type=simple;rgn=div1;q1=fitly%20spoken;singl
egenre=All;view=text;subview=detail;sort=occur;idno=lincoln4;node=linc
oln4%3A264
10   *Ibid.*

Kansas Act in 1854 had awakened him from, to use an apt phrase from Kant, his "dogmatic slumbers," in relationship to the Book of Proverbs. The principle is paramount; it must be maintained and cultivated with the greatest of zeal. So, it can be likened to the apples of 25:11. They are the word fitly spoken, which are surrounded and complemented by the setting of silver. The "setting givers" in the history of the United States are the Declaration and the Constitution. They, like the silver of 25:11, surround the apples. Just as the silver isn't the focus, but serves to bring attention to the apples, so the documents we reverence aren't the focus, but serve to bring attention to the apple in the center—the principle of "Liberty to All." Proverbs 25:11 helped give Lincoln an image, a picture, a biblical anchor to the concept of Liberty to All that had riveted his brain for almost seven years.

The irony of all of this was that when Alexander Stephens exhorted Lincoln at the end of 1860 in the words of Proverbs 25:11 to give a word "fitly spoken" to the nation, he hoped it would be a word that would heal the nation's wounds and mollify its tensions, a word which would cool the firebrands and ameliorate the harsh words flowing back and forth. Yet when Lincoln actually got around to letting the words of Proverbs 25:11 sink deeply into his mind, secession had already occurred and the hope for a "word fitly spoken" that would avert regional conflict had passed. Yet the Scripture still had its power, and Lincoln then used it to emphasize a central value for his life. Ultimately that value would become a cherished American value, even as we have struggled in the past 150 years to try to be faithful to the simple phrase "Liberty to All." But that concept might not have been framed so attractively and spoken so clearly had not Proverbs 25:11 entered into the equation.

Day Twenty-Six

TRYING A LITTLE KINDNESS

"Those who are kind reward themselves, but the
cruel do themselves harm," 11:17.

THE VERSE IS ARRESTING because it teaches us the
opposite of what we might initially believe. Isn't the result
or reward of kindness a benefit to *other* people? After all, we
always hear people saying, "I am indebted to the kindness of
X for enabling me to do what I have done." Then, looking at
the second colon of the verse, don't we believe that cruel people
fundamentally harm *others* and not themselves? The text doesn't
suggest that *every* reward of kindness is to the doer of an act, but
it does emphasize that kindness redounds to or boomerangs upon
the kind person, as well as cruelty upon one who does harm.

Kindness may bring rewards in two ways: either because,
as we often say, kindness is its own reward or because the author
of the proverb believes that kindness actually brings tangible
benefits to the doer of the act of kindness. This essay argues that

acts of kindness benefit the doer of the acts because these acts provide protection or shelter for the one receiving the kindness, and this shelter allows the recipient space to develop his/her life and creativity, which invariably will benefit the original, kind person.[1]

ON KINDNESS IN THE BIBLE

The balance of this essay focuses on the Hebrew word translated "kindness" and a story from early Christian literature on the transformative effect of kindness on a life. The word *hesed*, usually rendered "kindness," "loyalty," "goodness," "steadfast love," or "covenant faithfulness," appears more than 200 times in the Bible.[2] More than 1/2 of those are in the Psalms. An example is Ps. 136, a liturgical Psalm, where the *hesed* of God is celebrated in each of its 26 verses. It begins:

> "Oh give thanks to the Lord, for he is good;
>> For his *hesed* endures forever."
> Oh give thanks to the God of gods;
>> For his *hesed* endures forever," (Ps. 136:1-2).

The word is normally used of God's activity, but often, as in Prov. 11:17, it can describe human action. An important biblical

---

1 One other idea, which I don't explore here, is what you might call the "mental health" benefits of kindness. Practicing kindness tends to unclutter the life, thus giving wider scope to develop one's own healthy rhythms in life.

2 The classic study on *hesed* is Nelson Glueck's 1967 work, *Hesed in the Bible*. His basic point is that *hesed* needs to be understood as "conduct in accord with a mutual relationship of rights and duties, corresponding to a mutually obligatory relationship... principally: reciprocity, mutual assistance, sincerity, friendliness, brotherliness, duty, loyalty and love," p. 55.

text celebrating numerous divine virtues, including God's *hesed* is Ex. 34:6,

> "The Lord passed before him, and proclaimed,
> 'The Lord, the Lord,
> a God merciful and gracious,
> slow to anger,
> and abounding in *hesed* and faithfulness."

An equally famous text stressing the importance of doing *hesed* for humans is Micah 6:8,

> "He has told you, O mortal, what is good;
>   and what does the Lord require of you,
> but to do justice, and to love *hesed*,
>   and to walk humbly with your God?"

Kindness kounts. Cruelty cills.

A STORY FROM EARLY CHRISTIANITY

One of the most influential books from the early Christian era is St. Augustine's *Confessions*.[3] He wrote it at the close of the 4th century CE, around the time he was consecrated Bishop of Hippo in North Africa. The *Confessions* not only supplies us valuable information about his early life, but it provided a template or model for the genre of religious autobiography in late antiquity and the Middle Ages.[4]

---

3   Many excellent translations exist. The passage quoted below is taken from the translation by F. J Sheed, in the edition introduced by Peter Brown.
4   A helpful and accessible brief biographical sketch of his life is found here: http://en.wikipedia.org/wiki/Augustine_of_Hippo.

Augustine didn't officially make a profession of faith in Christ until he was about 33 years old, in 387 CE. Leading to that profession were a series of what one might call "mini-conversions," as he first was converted to philosophy as a 19 year-old, then to a certain brand of it (Manicheanism), then to a more refined philosophical system (Neo-Platonism) and finally to Catholic Christianity. One of the issues that stood in his way of adopting a Christian confession was the simplicity of the faith as practiced in rural North African congregations. In order to find Christianity attractive, Augustine needed a robust faith that was intellectually challenging and rewarding.

En route to finding such a faith, Augustine happened to accept a position teaching rhetoric in Milan, Italy, in the early 380s. One of his first acquaintances in that leading city of the late Roman Empire was Ambrose, Bishop of Milan. Ambrose was, as James O'Donnell says in his biography of Augustine,[5] from the highest classes in Rome, and he provided Augustine a method of interpreting Scripture through the lens of Neo-platonic philosophy. This lens or prism not only satisfied Augustine's intellectual longings but also provided the means for him to re-examine the creation story (Gen. 1) in the last few books of the *Confessions*. We look to the *Confessions* themselves to discover Augustine's first reaction to Ambrose when they met.

> "When therefore a message from Milan came to
> Rome, to the prefect, asking for a professor of
> Rhetoric for that city and arranging for public funds
> to cover the journey, I applied for the post... The
> prefect Symmachus approved of a public oration I

5   Excerpts from O'Donnell's *Augustine* (2005) are online. Dr. O'Donnell keeps an illuminating web site on Augustine at http://www9.georgetown.edu/faculty/jod/augustine.

delivered for the occasion, and sent me. So I came to Milan, to the bishop and devout servant of God, Ambrose, famed among the best men of the whole world...That man of God received me as a father, and as bishop welcomed my coming. I came to love him, not at first as a teacher of the truth, which I had utterly despaired of finding in Your church, but for his *kindness* towards me..."[6]

In Augustine's case, the kindness of Ambrose provided him a shelter and a place for intellectual experimentation, a place of welcoming as he tried to reconcile this new "reading" of the Christian faith with his own experience.

That, in a nutshell, is why I believe that *hesed* rewards one who practices it. You show kindness to someone. The recipient of kindness knows s/he is protected by the kindness. Feeling secure, the recipient of kindness can than explore, grow, question, and eventually come to a firmer and more secure location in the world. Then, as time passes, the protected person moves from a feeling of security to actually finding his or her own voice in the world. This voice often exceeds in scope and visibility that of original person who showed the kindness. And, what results? Well, the recipient feels s/he just wants to return the favor to the protector. Protector rewarded. Kindness comes back to reward the kind one.

The truth of this is evident in every walk of life but is particularly gratifying for teachers. For years a teacher labors, pouring heart and soul into students and material. You often feel, and you are probably right, that *nothing* seems to be "sinking in." At times you feel as if you are speaking in a soundproof phone

6   *Confessions* 5.13.

booth and the class of dazed faces is on the outside of the booth. But then, as years go by, one student and then another comes back to you. They remember few things of what you actually say, but they will never forget the kindness that you showed them. They remember the kindness because it provided them "space," or an opportunity to explore the confusing thoughts roiling their brains. Space or opportunity for discovery is of crucial importance in the unfolding of one's life.

So, the student comes back into the life of the teacher, often several years later, with his or her own training complete and a vision of their contribution to life. They are grateful for the kindness of the teacher, even though the specific lessons have been forgotten. The kind person has rewarded him/herself by having a loyal student, now in his or her prime, shaped by and grateful to the kind person.

I used to think that the following verse applied only to monetary gifts. Now I know it relates to kindness:

"Some give freely, yet grow all the richer;
        others withhold what is due, and only suffer
        want," Prov. 11:24.

It's not too late to show kindness to others. Some of the most satisfying opportunities to show kindness, and the subsequent rewards of kindness in my own life have *after* I have given up teaching in schools. And, I believe, more is still to come.

Day Twenty-Seven

EDUCATION AND PROVERBS 22:6

LOOKING CLOSELY AT THE WORDS OF THE VERSE

THE TRADITIONAL TRANSLATION of this verse is so-well known that it lulls us into intellectual complacency. Such a translation runs:

> "Bring up a child (train children) in the right way,
>> and when old, they will not stray" (NRSV; many
>> others are similar).

We *think* we know what the verse means, and so we politely listen to it and then dismiss it from our minds. We *think* it means that we should educate young people properly (maybe even in "God's way") and then they won't depart from it when older. But we have a bad conscience about this reading of the verse, because we know such a reading just isn't always true to life. People depart from "the way" all the time, despite the fact that they were raised by the most caring and conscientious parents. Children brought up in religious homes are on Death Rows in various states, including my own. Thus, the verse can become an occasion for recrimination, mutual accusation, judgmentalism, guilt, anguish and grief. And then we ignore the verse, provided we gave it much heed in the first place.

But the traditional translation just won't do. It doesn't do justice to the texture of the Hebrew words, the theory of education underlying the words or the developing notion of education we are adopting in our 21st century world.

A better translation is as follows:

> "Consecrate the youth according to what his way dictates; even when he becomes old, he will not depart from it."[1]

First, let's look at the words themselves. The first word, usually rendered "train" or "bring up" is actually a rare Hebrew verb, appearing fewer than 5X in the Bible. In other contexts it means to "dedicate" or "consecrate" a house or temple (Deut. 20:5; I Kings 8:63), and that kind of meaning ought not to escape us here. What one is doing in the nurturing of a child is actually the sacred act of dedication or consecration. Further, the Arabic noun underlying or running parallel to the Hebrew verb is "gums"—and hearkens back to the practice in that part of the world of anointing the gums of newborns with oil or dates, thus initiating the child to life and stimulating the sucking instinct.[2] Already in the careful study of the first word a picture of "education" is emerging. It is a sacred task; it is individually

---

1   Translation by Bruce K Waltke, *The Book of Proverbs*, 15—31, p 194.
2   *Ibid.*, p. 204, note 60.

applied.

The following words take us further. We are exhorted to consecrate "the youth." The direct object is a definite direct object in the Hebrew and isn't simply given as a general exhortation about "a child." A specific child is in view. Anticipating what I will say later in this essay, it is interesting that the 2004 Amendments to the most sweeping special education law in American history (the Individuals with Disabilities Education Act of 1975) stresses that the focus of developing an Individualized Education Program (IEP) is to work with "one child."[3] The Book of Proverbs is aware that the focus of education is not "youth" or "children" as such, but is the "one child." It may or may not take a village to raise this child, but the passage is unequivocal that only one individual is in view.

The rest of the first part of the verse (the first colon) confirms this. The sage is to consecrate the specific child in accordance with "his way" or "to what his way dictates." Historically the phrase "his way" has been taken to mean "God's way"—and thus the Book of Proverbs would be teaching that true education would be conforming a person to the dictates of a divine path laid out for the child.[4] But that translation, through grammatically possible, does not seem to fit as well into the flow of the text so far translated. A better reading of the "his way" is "the way of the child" or "youth." The entire verse before these words focuses on the child; why not continue to read the verse with that focus? By reading the text this way, a profound truth emerges. Education, to work, must be "child centered" or "fit for the child" or "appropriate to the needs of the individual, consecrated child."

---

3   http://www.ed.gov/parents/needs/speced/iepguide/index.html

4   A recent example of this interpretation is Tremper Longman III's *Proverbs*, pp. 404-05.

It isn't simply a curriculum that is written elsewhere, transported to teachers trained at "State U" and then poured into passive youthful containers. Education, in the Proverbs 22:6 way, is one that is based on the "child's way."

PROVERBS' EDUCATION AND OUR EDUCATION

Is public education today based on the principle of the "child's way?" Not by a long shot, even though educators today might occasionally mouth the words at the end of the last paragraph. Historically there was a sort of "standardized" education package, which would be evaluated by standardized tests, tests of intelligence, of competence in fields, of mastery. I was a product of this system, and I have often thought that it had more deficiencies than advantages. This still is the approach in the vast majority of school districts. Just recently, however, while consulting in Kansas, I learned that they are implementing a "Multi-Tiered System of Supports," which is fancy lingo for a system which increasingly recognizes that a goodly portion of students (I was told that about 20% was in view) needed "individualized" attention—that they just won't be able to learn in a "standardized" setting.[5]

But even more to the point of this essay is the development of special education law in the US, Canada and the UK over the last 35 years, a law which emphasizes the centrality of developing an "Individualized Educational Program" ("Plan" in the UK and Canada) for *each* disabled student. That is, a cornerstone of disability education in our day is that each student's learning needs and physical/mental challenges have to be taken into

---

5   A description of this Kansas-based program is http://www.ksde.org/Default. aspx?tabid=204

account in crafting an educational program to maximize their potential. Indeed, such a plan has been held mandatory by the courts, as part of a student's FAPE (Free Appropriate Public Education).

If special education law says that *each* student needs an IEP; if a consensus of educators may be leading to the notion that perhaps 20% of students can't learn in the "traditional" environment; if Proverbs, read the way I have presented it, stresses the centrality of bringing a child up in "his way" (i.e., the means best suited for the child to learn), why don't we implement something like this *for every student*? Why shouldn't *each* student, and *each* learner, get an IEP? Why shouldn't we take the time to discover in what ways a specific child, each specific child, learns best and then tailor material to this child's need?

A quick answer, of course, is costs. People talk about costliness before they even think of a proper answer to the question. They say, 'It might just cost too much to spend time figuring out how each person learns and how to maximize his/her talents.' I, however, have a different take on it. Since most people spend decades trying to *ignore* the effects of their education, others spend many years afterwards trying to *undo* its effects, and others spend countless thousands of dollars in therapy trying to figure out who they are, why not spend the "up front" money to "consecrate" students in "their own" way? The world, my friends, would be grateful—in about 40 years.

Proverbs has many verses which seem to emphasize that education or training in wisdom is a "standardized" package. But then you have 22:6, which, read in the way I have read it, opens the door to a host of questions that never seemed to be foremost in the minds of my teachers. I believe that Proverbs 22:6 can be the philosophical cornerstone of a 21st century educational revolution, and that the most useful task for school teachers and districts to engage in is to discover what each child's "way" of learning is. It certainly would take some time, but the quality of learning that would emerge from those schools would astonish us.

I have written more about this in a web essay, "An IEP for Everyone."[6]

---

6 http://www.drbilllong.com/CurrentEventsVIII/IEP.html. The book I am currently writing, tentatively titled, *Teaching and Learning in America: 2010*, explores these ideas in greater depth.

Chapter Twenty-Eight

PROVERBS 16:20 AND THE REDISCOVERY
OF GENIUS AND TALENT

"Those who are attentive to a matter will prosper,
and happy are those who trust in the Lord,"
16:20.

THIS ESSAY WAS STIMULATED by a May 1, 2009 *New York Times* column by David Brooks. Entitled "Genius: The Modern View," Brooks argues that current literature on talent and genius rejects the romantic view of genius as someone possessed of a divine spark or capacity exceeding that of "normal" people and adopts the more optimistic position that talent/genius primarily results from the concerted application of effort and practice in an intelligent way over the space of many years. In other words, in recent literature we have emerging a more "democratic" view of genius. Anyone, perhaps, can be a genius, as long as s/he puts enough quality effort into something.

Two of the leading proponents of this newer view have published books on the subject in the past year. Geoff Colvin, a writer for *Fortune Magazine*, argues in *Talent is Overrated*[1] that the key to maximum talent development is what he calls "deliberate practice." He defines this as a state somewhere between work and play, where a person carefully cultivates him/herself over a long period of time, with special attention to pushing oneself slightly beyond one's limits every time, so that one may eventually extend one's limits. In a video explaining the book, he gave the example of the comedian Chris Rock who, in preparing for a widely publicized comedy routine, would begin the process several months in advance by having "gigs" in less well-known environments, where he could gradually "try out" material, build on what works, and finally achieve a stunning performance where 100% of his jokes were "home runs." Thus, the key, for Colvin, in developing extreme talent is to identify what is meant by "better" performance and then developing a method to get there. Others who adopt this position say that it takes around 10,000-15,000 hours of effort to get to this level of accomplishment [5-8 years of "full-time" work on the subject].

Daniel Coyle reaches similar conclusions in his recent book *The Talent Code*.[2] His subtitle gives his thesis in a nutshell: "Greatness isn't born. It is grown." Coyle comes at the subject, however, from a slightly different angle than Colvin. He decided to do his research by traveling to nine places on earth that have produced a disproportionate share of amazingly talented people in various activities. One of these places, for example, was the Pabao Little League, Willemstad, Curacao, whose team has

1   Portfolio Hardcover (October 2008).
2   Bantam (April 2009).

ended up in the finals or semi-finals of the Little League World Series in Williamsport, PA for six of the past eight years.[3] Coyle argues that at least three things seem to be uniquely important to cultivate this kind of talent. He calls them "deep practice," "mature coaching" and "ignition." Deep practice emphasizes deliberate mastery. It means taking 90 seconds to complete a tennis stroke that takes one second; it means playing musical notes in a composition so slowly and deliberately that if passersby can recognize the tune you are playing, you are playing too quickly. That is, Coyle argues that talent/genius is attained by mastering the most detailed aspects of a skill, practicing them over and over very slowly so that the skill can be maximally demonstrated.

But talent development takes more than simply practice or application, for Coyle. It needs the "ignition" of the heart, or the great desire or ambition of the student/learner to be great, and it requires mature coaching, preferably by those who have been coaching for more than a decade.

One of the reasons, in my judgment, for this new view of genius or maximal talent development, is the increased attention devoted in scholarship to the functioning of the brain. Coyle, for example, specifically points to the neurophysiology of the brain as motivating his work—and he isolates the importance of myelin, the fatty tissue insulating nerves, to create and maintain increased strength and speed of electrical signals throughout the nervous system. Scholarly thinking on talent and genius today, then, is focused more on the specific, identifiable steps that everyone can take to maximize the self rather than a "spark" or "innate talent" that only a few have.

3   A list of the other places, with brief descriptions of what he found in each location—such as the cultivation of writers, pop music, skateboarders, soccer players, is found here: http://thetalentcode.com/2009/03/30/pabao-little-league/

PROVERBS 16:20 AND GENIUS OR TALENT

The issue of what produces extremely talented people is probably more complex than what has been presented by either of these researchers, and the brief summary just given begs lots of questions,[4] but this work on talent and genius get us on a track to understand some elements of the Book of Proverbs. In fact, all three elements of "deep practice," "ignition" and "mature coaching" are foundational in Proverbs for the life of wisdom. I treated "ignition" in the second essay; and the book of Proverbs is so replete with the importance of following the sages that nothing more needs to be said. In the remainder of this essay, I will touch briefly upon the "Proverbial" equivalent to "deep" or "deliberate" practice—what Proverbs calls "attentiveness."

The first stanza of Proverbs 16:20 allows for several translations because of the generality and inclusiveness of some of the terms. Literally we have, "The one who is attentive (or has insight) into a matter (or word or thing) will find good (or prosperity or benefit)..." Rather than trying to figure out whether it is more likely that *dabar*, most frequently translated "word" in the Bible, is actually "word" or "thing" or "matter," it might be better to allow the full semantic scope of *dabar* to be on display, and thus let the word "play" with us as we try to understand it. Thus, the linguistic range of the first colon can be as wide as "one who has insight into a word (of a wise person)" to "one who

4   For example, is there a difference between "talent" and "genius"? How is a word we use all the time to describe gifted people, "brilliance," related to all of this? Then, when all is said and done, isn't there still a recognition that some people don't only have an "ignition" or strong desire for a field or activity but are gifted almost beyond measure in that activity? For example, Orlando Magic Center Dwight Howard, for example, has a physique that only comes around once in a decade in sports...

is attentive to a thing or matter" (broadly construed). Why not swim widely in this sea, since we are really given no reason to confine our explorations narrowly?

The word translated "attentive" in 16:20 is the Hebrew word *maskil*, a word translated as "insight" in 1:3. But the inclination to translate it as "attentive" is derived from its use in Prov. 21:11 and Dan. 9:13. In the latter verse, the relevant phrase, including the word *maskil*, is rendered "have regard for his truth" in the NRSV. The emphasis in the verse is on the people of Israel's intense personal dedication to Yahweh's truth as a means of escaping judgment. Then, in Prov. 21:11, a leading translation has:

> "Through fining a mocker, the gullible becomes
>   wise, and through paying attention (*behasekil*) to
>   a wise person he gains knowledge."[5]

This "paying attention" to a wise person is elsewhere clarified by a phrase such as "one who walks with a wise person" (14:20) or "one who treasures up wisdom" (2:1-4). Thus, even if we can't see all the elements of "deep practice" clearly spelled out in Proverbs, the emphasis on attentiveness, on focused assiduity, now takes on a deeper significance. Such a person will find "good" (*tov*). That simple Hebrew word is full of such deep significance, and its linguistic range covers everything from earthly prosperity to a divine satisfaction at the end of the creative process in Gen. 1.

Thus, an expanded translation of 16:20 is, "Those who give focused attention to matters before them will reap all kinds of

---

5   Waltke, Bruce, *Proverbs 15-31*, p. 161,

good things." Thus, be attentive in all you do, take time to store up wisdom, take time to walk quietly with the wise, and good will follow. It is almost too frighteningly simple to believe.

Day Twenty-Nine

PROVERBS 16:23 AND THE HEART'S GENERATIVE CAPACITY

"The mind of the wise makes their speech judicious
and adds persuasiveness to their lips," 16:23
(traditional translation).

SINCE I BELIEVE there is a lot at stake in a careful translation of this verse, I will begin with that issue.

REFLECTING ON THE TRANSLATION OF 16:23

The translation of the verse just given is from the New Revised Standard Version. If we were simply to stay with these words, we would have a pleasant-enough proverb, consistent with many others, about the way that wisdom affects speech. A wise person speaks well; that is a consistent message of Proverbs (see 25:11; 15:23). But when we look more closely at the Hebrew

265

words, we see that an alternative translation is not only more alluring but also is truer to the text. The Geneva Bible comes closest to the translation I will use:

> "The heart of the wise teaches his mouth,
> And adds learning to his lips."

But we can take the text even further. The first word of the Hebrew text is *leb*, which is normally translated "heart." So, let's keep it translated that way. By so translating it, we connect it with the other "heart" verses of Proverbs, the principal one of which is 4:23 (see day five above). "Above all things, guard your heart..." Then, the text uses a verb whose noun form is a common word in Proverbs for "prudence." My rendering of the first colon, thus, is "The heart of the wise leads to prudence in the mouth..." In other words, the first part of the verse emphasizes the *way or manner* in which one speaks. The wise person's heart leads him or her to speak prudently.

The second colon emphasizes the *content* of the speech— learning. Since the NRSV and other versions translate the word *leqah* as "persuasiveness" rather than "learning" here, and since the difference seems important to me, let me pause on the word *leqah* for a moment. Bruce Waltke, the most thorough commentator on Proverbs in English (his two-volume work exceeds 1200 pages), recognizes that *leqah* can be translated two ways in the Old Testament: "learning the inherited tradition or persuasiveness."[1] He opts for the latter here and in 16:21 (where it also appears), without giving an explanation of why he believes it is a good translation.

---

1   *The Book of Proverbs, 15-31*, p. 29.

The word *leqah* only appears nine times in the Bible, and six of these are in Proverbs. The non-Proverbs usages clearly indicate a connection with teaching or instruction. For example, when Moses recites his famous song to the Israelites, shortly before his death, he begins:

"May my teaching (*leqah*) drop like the rain
  my speech condense like the dew," Deut 32:2.

That teaching is a good translation for *leqah* here is evident when we continue to read the song; Moses starts "instructing" the people about God's dealing with the people in 32:4.

The same might be said about its appearance in Job 11:4. Zophar, one of Job's interlocutors, speaks in Job 11. In contrast to the first speeches of Eliphaz and Bildad, Zophar starts right in by criticizing Job. He states Job's contention or argument in v. 4, and then proceeds to demolish that argument (in his own mind). He says,

"For you say, 'My conduct (*leqah*) is pure,
  and I am clean in God's sight."

The NRSV translation is not a bad one, for Job has been appealing to the purity of how he has lived. But his life is a combination of his righteous actions and his words/teaching. A rendering of *leqah* as "persuasiveness" here would be far from the mark.

The translation of *leqah* as persuasiveness is justified in its appearance in Proverbs 7:21. There the loose woman has been trying for several verses to entice the young man, the one who is supposed to be pursuing wisdom, to follow her. The text says:

"With much seductive (*leqah*) speech she persuades
　　him;
　　with her smooth talk she compels him."

But a few other instances of its appearance in Proverbs clearly favor the "instruction" or "learning" or "teaching" translation. For example, in 1:5, the important preamble to the book, we discover that the purpose of the Proverbs, among other things, can be stated as follows:

"Let the wise also hear and gain in learning
　　(*leqah*).."

This is the translation of *leqah* here in both the NRSV and Waltke. Significant for me is the parallel phrasing to 16:23. We have the same verb "add" or "gain" and the same noun "learning." Thus, if we render it "learning" in 1:5, we ought to so render it in 16:23. Or, to put it differently, the burden is on those who would render it "persuasiveness" in 16:23. The Book of Proverbs would be a bit weak in its appeal to the wise if the major benefit would be to add to their persuasiveness. Persuasiveness certainly is important, but learning is the foundation of life for Proverbs. Let's go with "learning" or "instruction" or "teaching" for *leqah* in Proverbs 16:23.

WHAT IS AT STAKE IN THE TRANSLATION

I have taken more trouble with the translation of this verse than any other because of what I consider to be at stake in the verse. In short, the verse is talking about the generative power of the heart—for learning. Most of our attention on Proverbs, and almost all the reading I have done on the book, stresses the importance of mastering the tradition of the sages or the wisdom passed on from parent to child. *That* is how the wise person learns. Wisdom has a definite content, beginning with the fear of the Lord, and it is to be expressed in proper forms and in suitable circumstances. One might get the impression through this reading of Proverbs that learning and gaining in wisdom or knowledge is completely dependent on attentiveness to the wisdom of others, of the inherited tradition. But the liberating idea in this verse is that the heart of the wise person, in *addition to the tradition of the sages*, is the source of learning for the wise one. That is, just as the heart of a person pumps blood, and various organs of our body generate something from more basic building blocks, so our heart is a generator of knowledge.

If we truly let this thought sink in, we realize that we ourselves or, to put it slightly differently, those who have hearts dedicated to wisdom, are generators of learning. Certainly it is true that all great thinkers who conceive of themselves as standing in a tradition of interpretation, whether it is a religious or a secular tradition, see themselves as standing on the shoulders of their predecessors.[2] Many would say that they are simply trying to be faithful to the tradition, to be true to those who have come before them. But, in fact, by sifting the tradition and the teachings, by trying to master not simply the content but the modes of thought,

2 An eloquent defense of tradition, from the perspective of theological thought, is the late Jaroslav Pelikan's 1983 Jefferson Lecture on the Humanities, which was published as *The Vindication of Tradition* (Yale, 1986). According to the website of St. Vladimir's Orthodox Seminary (he converted from Lutheranism to Orthodoxy in 1998), Pelikan was especially fond of a line from Goethe's *Faust*: "What you have as heritage, take now as task, and thus you will make it your own." Quoted here: http://www.svots.edu/News/Recent/2006-0513-pelikan/

the gaps between thoughts, the unfilled interstices of cogitation, creative thinkers add to the tradition. Tradition is a living, supple concept, as alive as river flowing peacefully or tumultuously down its channel to the sea.

The interpreter of the tradition, then, is herself or himself an active constructor of the tradition. How can that be? Because of the person's *leb* or heart. The person is fully committed to applying the resources of the tradition, in combination with the heart, to interpret, internalize and live the tradition in the present. But if you already have a modicum of wisdom as you apply yourself to that learning process, then the heart, as it were, teaches you in the night.

I am arguing, then, that according to Proverbs there are two sources of knowledge for the wise person: the traditions of the sages and the language of the heart. In so arguing, I am struck by the similarity of this thought to one in the Psalms:

"I bless the Lord who gives me counsel;
In the night also my heart instructs me," Ps. 16:7.

Not only are these words consistent with what we are increasingly discovering about the role of dreams and the functions of the brain, but it is true to our experience. We learn from the tradition (the Lord; the sages) and we learn from our hearts.

CONCLUSION

The conclusion that we reach is that the heart of the wise person is an incredibly valuable resource. It not only becomes the locus of what we might call "study knowledge" which, when put together faithfully becomes wisdom, but is also the place where new connections are made between various sources of knowledge and where a personal "angle" on the learning is established. No wonder we are to guard it above all things we guard (4:23). I like to think that this second source of learning—the heart—also helps organize our thoughts, make them more crisp and clear, and helps them be so refracted through our personality and humor, through everything that is in us, that we as it were become living exemplars of a vibrant tradition. We become not simply boats, as it were, carried on the river of the tradition, but we become like tributaries of that great river, joining it, mingling with it, adding to its color and temperature and depth, and flowing jointly to the sea. Such is the power and the generative capacity of the wise heart.

Day Thirty

PROVERBS IN BRIEF

IMMERSING ONESELF IN THE BOOK of Proverbs has both a desirable and disconcerting effect on us. On the one (desirable) hand, we realize that the insights from this ancient text, which have showered themselves on us, are so rich and useful that they can provide the basis for wise and good living. On the other (disconcerting) hand, the insights have also started to flow with such regularity and power that I now see I may need to write a "30 More Days With Proverbs"—type of book. This second book would caress the text with even more care, linking proverb with proverb as we probe further into the life of wisdom.

We work in life and we talk about work. We live and we talk about life. Proverbs is a book which gives me a language to talk about life. It certainly doesn't broach every important area of life (see the last "day" for further reflection on this), but it yields enough light on enough important subjects to make it worthwhile to spend loads of time with it. I am convinced, as

I get older, that most learning which "sticks" with us is gained one sentence at a time. Proverbs is a book which believes that every sentence uttered is precious, and that learning happens one precept at a time.

This chapter will briefly introduce several more proverbs which require much more attention that I can give them here...

THE TEST OF PRAISE

"The crucible is for silver and the furnace is for gold,
so a person is tested by being praised," 27:21.

Woody Hayes, the famed football coach of the Ohio State Buckeyes in the 1950s and 1960s, was asked why he favored the run over the pass when all major football programs were increasingly going to the air. His attitude was philosophical. "If," he said, "we put the ball in the air, three things can happen, two of which are bad. The ball can be intercepted or fall incomplete. If, however, we stay on the ground, only one bad thing can happen, a fumble."

It isn't my purpose to criticize the logic of the late coach; suffice it to say for our purposes that praise, the subject of 27:21, functions like Woody Hayes' forward pass. When you are praised, two bad things and only one good thing can happen to you. The good thing is that if the person means it and you accept it graciously, both giver and recipient of praise are enriched.

Two bad things, the "shadow side" of praise, can happen when praise comes our way. Praise can be said insincerely, and it can be received in the wrong spirit. If it is said insincerely, and the person praising you really has another agenda (such as to get your money or something else), then the possibilities of deception, including self-deception, are enhanced. If it is said sincerely and you receive it incorrectly, by letting it "go to your head," then it has harmed you more than helped you.

Anyone who is a fan of men's college basketball knows that the worst thing that can happen for the team is to be ranked No. 1 in December or January. It *never* lasts. There are several reasons for this, but one of them certainly is that players get the impression that the national ranking entitles them to something—as if the other team is going to roll over and play dead. In fact, it often earns you the opposite—teams are "gunning" for you.

Praise, therefore, is a dangerous thing, a double-edged sword. It can often do more to get a person off-track than to keep them on-track. Yet, we know that praise is necessary, too, because it tells you, the laborer, that someone else recognizes your worth and contribution. How do you handle the "test" of praise? Or do you even see it as a test? "A profound psychological observation," is what Biblical scholar Roland Murphy calls this proverb.[1]

SMALL QUANTITY, GREAT VALUE

"If you have found honey, eat only enough for you,
　　or else, having too much, you will vomit it.
Let your foot seldom be in your neighbor's house,
　　Otherwise the neighbor will
　　become weary of you and hate you," 25:16-17.

"It is not good to eat much honey,
or to seek honor on top of honor," 25:27.

Though the verses are linked by the notion of restraint

1　*Proverbs*, p. 209.

or self-control, they each have their own genius. The honey envisioned in verse 16 is wild honey, which a person might come upon by chance. Honey is of great importance as an immediate energy boost in a sun-drenched desert climate. One might think that when you come on it by chance that you ought to take all of it that you can. You may not know when you will get more food; you aren't taking it from anyone (since it is wild); it tastes so good. Why not just indulge? Because even good things taken in too great proportion end up hurting more than helping us. Mae West may have said, "Too much of a good thing is never enough," but that philosophy fits Hollywood more than intelligent living.

A literal translation of the second verse (25:17) is "let your foot be precious" in your neighbor's house. It is similar to the idea expressed in another proverb—that rising early and blessing your neighbor in a loud voice will be considered a curse. The idea is that restrained presence, like the restrained consumption of honey, will yield better results for you.

The older I get the more I want just to "give a glimpse" of myself to people. Staying too long at a party, as well as overstaying your welcome as guests, can leave people with a sense of sourness when they think of you. Dole yourself out in small dollops; only consume small amounts; don't seek much praise or honor.

MUDDYING THE WATERS

"Like a muddied spring or a polluted fountain
   are the righteous who give way before the
   wicked," 25:26.

Life has its battles, battles with people, with systems, with understanding, with health, with having enough to live on, with trying to find and keep love. In each of the struggles in which we engage there are the dual tensions of giving up or taking the struggle to completion. Sometimes, or maybe even often, not much is at stake. Yet life is a series of struggles. It is easier, at times, just to capitulate, especially if there appears to be little choice in the matter. But often it is better not to capitulate to things, especially if there appears to be a dimension of considerable evil, major humiliation or loss of dignity in the process. By not taking steps to stand up to evil, or the wicked, one is becoming a muddied stream or polluted fountain. Indeed, that is what it feels like when you acquiesce when you know it would have been better for you to confront a situation. We acquiesce, we give in, because we don't want to take the effort to change things; because we feel it isn't important; or, more subtly, because that is the way we have always confronted life's difficulties. This proverb lends not simply massive encouragement to us in struggling against injustices but it explains why *we* feel so dirty when we yield to someone else's improper desires.

SELLING OUT

"To show partiality is not good —
  yet for a piece of bread a person may do wrong,"
  28:21.

In the Land of the Free, people are owned. More than 140 years after the elimination of slavery in this country, most people still live in chains. We rise early, rush to work, come home late, and barely have time for cultivating the things that truly matter to us. We may not think of ourselves as "owned," but in fact that is our life.

A potential implication of this fact concerns me. If we are, largely, owned by another, then our opinions, ideas and public statements are often shaped by the body or individual that "owns" us. When we make those statements, we don't often represent who our owner is or whose "water" we are carrying. As a result, everything from the public airwaves to scientific journals are subject to being hijacked by people whose major concerns are not the good of the public or the discoveries of science, but the promotion of a named (or frequently unnamed) client's interests. Assuming that Proverbs is right—"yet for a piece of bread a person may do wrong"—then we have the reality of people willfully representing things in various forums that really aren't good for that forum but reflect the interests of one who would want to control it or get some benefit from it.

This issue is far from abstract. Medical schools and continuing education events are re-evaluating the way that large corporate donations, especially from pharmaceutical companies, might affect the way that medicine is taught and practiced. It makes one wonder sometimes if there ever is a possibility that the public good, rather than a series of private goods, can be identified and honored. Proverbs warns us of the reality—people will do wrong for a piece of bread. If people do that, they certainly will do wrong for $100,000 a year...

UPENDING THE COMMUNITY

"Scoundrels concoct evil, and their speech is like a
    scorching fire.
A perverse person spreads strife,
    And a whisperer separates close friends.

The violent entice their neighbors,

And lead them in a way that is not good," 16:27-29.

You can go to several universities to study "community building." People write books on how to build a community. Everyone seems to want a community that functions well and that is a pleasant place to live. Yet, the Book of Proverbs is fascinated by those who tear down the community. Proverbs isn't afraid to identify these people and call them what they truly are— scoundrels. They are the mockers or scoffers in other passages, but here they are scoundrels. Their work in the public sphere is reminiscent of whisperers in the private—who even manage to insinuate themselves between close friends and break them apart. There are those who delight in breaking something down, in making all the rest of the world suffer. Perhaps they want the rest of the community to share what goes on in their (i.e., the scoundrel's) life each day.

The Book of Proverbs is concerned to build a moral and wise structure of living for the individual, but it realizes that this life must be lived out in the context of a community. Thus, a community that creates and maintains the conditions for wisdom's flourishing is the goal of Proverbs. But in order for that kind of community to live, certain types of people must be identified and dealt with. Scoffers, scoundrels, hotheads and others (we *do* need another book, to define all these more precisely, don't we?) need to be isolated so that they cannot do any more damage to the people. Wisdom seeking, then, is not simply about living a wise life and controlling the self; it also concerns the establishment of a community which creates the conditions for this wisdom to flourish. What is the scope or range of that community? Can it be a town, state or nation? Most certainly. Thus, Proverbs gives us a tall order indeed.

Many more proverbs could be discussed. I end here, however, with the hope that you see the value not simply of wisdom for your life but of the importance of disciplining yourself to follow the path of wisdom. Proverbs doesn't just contain wise or witty sayings; it contains crucial knowledge for a satisfying life.

Day Thirty-One

CODA—SO MANY PROVERBS, SO LITTLE TIME

L EST YOU THINK that the preceding expositions "exhaust" the Book of Proverbs, I have written this closing chapter to indicate how much more there is to understand about this ancient classic. But, lest you think that the Book of Proverbs is all you need in life, I close this chapter with mention of some important topics that Proverbs *doesn't* cover.

ADDITIONAL THOUGHTS

When we probe any subject, it invites us to enter it more deeply. Study a Victorian-era home. Before long you want to know all the differences among Second Empire, Greek Revival, Queen Anne, Italianate, Eastlake, Victorian Vernacular and several other styles. You want to know all the words that define the homes, so that every piece of Queen Anne gingerbread has a name, and every bar of Second Empire cresting is sympathetically

281

described. Or, take flowers. You learn the "easy" ones, the ones in everyone's garden. But then there are wildflowers, differing by region, and wildly exotic flowers, and bushes, shrubs, trees, the things that lodge in trees, flowers and bushes, the things that threaten those beautiful accoutrements of life, and all of a sudden you are learning to describe life with a richness, precision and appreciation that you never knew existed. You realize that you have been living "on the surface" of life for so long, and you discover that there is life, abundant life, when you plumb depths.

So it is with Proverbs. Once you grant that Proverbs possesses psychological depth, you begin to see depth elsewhere in the book. Proverbs becomes, among other things, a book of psychological enrichment. Look at Prov. 27:11,

"Be wise, my child, and make my heart glad,
    so that I may answer whoever reproaches me."

Is Proverbs hinting here at a connection between encouragement and ability to "make it" in the world by being able to answer a reproacher? Is there wisdom in making another's heart glad? What are the means by which one does this? Other Scriptures talk about wine which gladdens the heart (Ps. 104:15), but that probably isn't what is in view here. In any case, we are plunged into worlds of psychological depth because we already believe that Proverbs takes us to those levels.

Then there are a bundle of additional individual proverbs that tend to leap off the page at us and clamor for recognition and exposition. Among them are:

"The wicked flee when no one pursues,

but the righteous are as bold as a lion," 28:1.

In what does that boldness consist? When should one "run into" the strong tower of the Lord (18:10), and when should one stand without fear and confront opposition?

"Wise warriors are mightier than strong ones,
    and those who have knowledge than those who
    have strength," 24:5.

Shouldn't this be emblazoned on the walls of Fort Jackson SC or Fort Benning GA, and shouldn't it be incumbent on trainers or other military personnel to show how they are making warriors *wise* as well as *strong*?

"He who finds a wife finds a good thing,
    and obtains favor from the Lord," 18:22.

How about "Proverbs and Dating" or "How to find a Good Wife"? Proverbs might become a best seller.

"Whoever pursues righteousness and kindness
    will find life and honor," 21:21.

Tell me how, and I will be first in line.

"To watch over mouth and tongue is to keep out of
    trouble," 21:23.

Amen.

"There is gold, and abundance of costly stones;

but the lips informed by knowledge are a
precious jewel," 20:15.

This is one of the most precious proverbs of all to me, and is the thing toward which I aspire. What are lips informed by knowledge? How do we get them? Care for them? Use them? Thinking about this verse will return us to the Book of Proverbs in general, to read it again and again.

OTHER THEMES

But Proverbs is more than just a series of individual aphorisms, precious as they are. It gives thoughtful advice and arresting observations about topics of importance for life, topics that I didn't have time to consider in this book. No study of justice and injustice is complete without examining Proverbs. What does it mean for our lives when it says:

"Those who forsake the law praise the wicked,
    but those who keep the law struggle against
    them," 28:4?

Is the act of keeping the law a sufficient struggle against the wicked or is there much more? Maybe some boldness as a lion (28:1)? But the next verse gives us hope:

"The evil do not understand justice,
    but those who seek the Lord understand it
    completely," 28:5.

Life is about justice and injustice, about the wise and

foolish, about the just and the wicked, about how to confront all of these things and people. Proverbs is not the charter for an eremitical community.

Proverbs' concept of justice is a visual one. That is, just as the Book of Proverbs draws on life experiences (looking in a reflecting pool; handling a dog; seeing a crippled person) to formulate its wisdom, so the concept of justice is, I believe, defined by the practical experience of weighing goods for purchase. In four passages, the author talks about unjust weights (11:1; 16:11; 20:10, 23). An example is:

> "Differing scales are an abomination to the Lord,
>   and false scales are not good," 20:23.

I think the fact of seeing, and maybe experiencing, the "short end" of an unjust measurement fuels the concept of justice in this book. But it invites lots more investigation. Especially important would be the connection between the word injustice and "abomination." The latter word appears 19 times in Proverbs, is an especially strong word, and therefore ought to be examined with care. What else is an abomination? To whom (people or God)?

> "One who justifies the wicked and one who
>   condemns the righteous are both alike an
>   abomination to the Lord," 17:15.

Another theme of central importance to Proverbs is the treatment of the poor. Proverbs is aware of, and doesn't really have sympathy for, a certain kind of poor person—those who are poor through their own sluggardness (the Oxford English

Dictionary also has "sluggardy" and "sluggardry," but calls both of these words "obsolete"). But so sympathetic is Proverbs to the plight of the poor that it has to conclude that most of the poor are in that condition through no fault of their own. Thus, the book can say:

> "Those who mock the poor insult their Maker,
> those who are glad at calamity will not go
> unpunished," 17:5.

Many verses on poverty and treating the poor are inviting:

> "One who augments wealth by exorbitant interest
> gathers it for another who is kind to the poor," 28:8.

Some are statements that themselves need little commentary:

> "The poor use entreaties, but the rich answer
> roughly," 18:23.

> "If the poor are hated even by their kind,
> how much more are they shunned by their
> friends!" 19:7.

There are more than 40 verses on wealth and poverty in Proverbs; this makes it among the most discussed issues in the book. Certainly, it deserves lots of our attention.

Then there are just some verses that you make you want to stop, mull over and convene a discussion group:

"Bread gained by deceit is sweet,

> but afterward the mouth will be filled with
> gravel," 20:17.

What, friends, are "gravel-filling" experiences for people? For you?

WHAT PROVERBS LACKS

I remember an occasion 33 years ago as if it was yesterday. I was taking a class at Episcopal Divinity School in Cambridge, MA. I wasn't a student there, but I had privileges to take courses at any of the eight theological schools in the Boston area because I was a student at one of them. The professor, a New Testament scholar, was asking us about our perception of "strengths and weaknesses" in Christianity. He shared his own thoughts and asked for ours. Several students shared their "problems" with Christianity. At that time I was a rather committed Evangelical, and I answered the question, "Christianity has no weaknesses, no vulnerabilities." That response also reflected my attitude to the Bible at that time. I believed not only that the Bible was a perfect book but that it had everything necessary to guide us to a good and meaningful life.

It took me quite a while to realize that the Bible itself isn't a complete book of life and that certain books of the Bible were more valuable than others. For quite a while I would have denied that Romans or the Gospels were more valuable than Nahum or Obadiah. Why? Because all Scripture was equally inspired by God. But I gradually abandoned that approach because it just didn't seem true to the text.

My "new" approach, then, was to look at individual

Scriptural books as offering their own perspectives or "takes" on life, perspectives that were true. They were not, however, the "whole truth." So, as we leave Proverbs, it is good to see what Proverbs *doesn't* do. First, it doesn't have a very robust conception of family life or marital relationships. We are told repeatedly that it is better to live in peace than with a contentious woman, and some might still chuckle at that kind of observation today. But no emphasis is given to how to make family life work or the way to cultivate and practice wisdom in the context of family.

Again, Proverbs doesn't probe the idea of friendship in any depth. It does have more here than it does on marriage, however. For example, we have:

"A friend loves at all times,
    and kinsfolk are born to share adversity," 17:17.

And,

"Iron sharpens iron,
    and one persons sharpens the wits of another," 27:17,

but the latter isn't presented in the context of friendship, and the former doesn't receive much development. Then there are verses that are a bit enigmatic on the subject, such as:

"Do not forsake your friend or the friend of your
    parent;
do not go to the house of your kindred in the day of
    your calamity," 27:10.

What might that mean?

Likewise, despite Proverbs' emphasis on right and just conduct, it has no real theology of hospitality or welcoming people. It has no philosophy of what we might call domestic life or the home. Well, neither do lots of other books, but Proverbs places so much emphasis on right education and training that you think there might be some things to say about how to welcome people into your home.

Then, in the realm of ideas or institutions important to all people or beloved of the people of Israel, Proverbs is also lacking. It has nothing about death, for example, other than a few verses such as the following:

"There is a way that seems right to a person,
    but its end is the way to death," 14:12.

Or, in describing the seductive speech of the loose woman and its effect on a young man, Proverbs says,

"He is like a bird rushing into a snare,
    not knowing that it will cost him his life," 7:23.

There is a lot of emphasis on how a wise person lives, but not much on how a wise person dies.

Certain central theological doctrines are also missing or downplayed in Proverbs. No mention is made of the Levitical system of sacrifice; the law is mentioned but no laws are stressed; little emphasis is placed on purity or a pure life. Finally, nothing is made of a "personal relationship" with God or the importance of spiritual disciplines, such as prayer. Proverbs primarily probes the educational task and the way that wisdom can be learned, cultivated and put to good use in life.

CONCLUSION

The Book of Proverbs, then, doesn't describe all of life. No book can. But it takes one concept, wisdom, an idea of diamond-like value, and holds it up to the jeweler's loupe of everyday living. With the loupe, which magnifies the stone, the jeweler can see the object in ways that the naked human eye cannot.

Or, maybe it is better to say that life is the diamond, and wisdom is the jeweler's loupe, which examines life carefully, exposing its finest faults, and then tries to "improve" them with skillful manipulation. The end product is a wise person, a person who has mastered life and can navigate the potential difficulties that come along. The wise person can do this because s/he has so honed the principles of wisdom that knowledge, insight, and even patience is easy. Most of us still have a long way to go to get to that situation. But since the rewards are great ("honor and glory and life"), there is no task more urgent and compelling. Seek wisdom and the life of wisdom. Everything else is commentary.

INDEX OF SCRIPTURAL REFERENCES

About the Author

Dr. William Long is a writer and consultant living in the Pacific Northwest. In the 25 years after receiving his Ph.D. in the History of Religions from Brown University, he pursued six different work venues: professor of religion and humanities, editorial writer for a major American daily newspaper, pastor of a large urban congregation, professor of history and government, litigation attorney, and professor of law. In addition to his own writing and learning, he now consults with individuals and boards of directors to enable superior levels of personal and company performance. He has written more than a dozen books and 4,000 online essays which you may read at www.drbilllong. com on subjects ranging from autism and Shakespeare to the study of words and legal history. Twice he has placed second in the National Spelling Bee; once he won a third. He has studied 11 languages and uses them to glean rare and valuable insights from texts ancient and modern. For more information visit him online at

www.drbilllong.com

3854454

Made in the USA